An
Introduction to
Legal
Reasoning

T0056028

An Introduction to Legal Reasoning

EDWARD H. LEVI

With a Foreword by
FREDERICK SCHAUER

The University of Chicago Press
CHICAGO & LONDON

EDWARD H. LEVI (1911–2000) *was attorney general of the United States from 1975 to 1977, president of the University of Chicago, and dean of the University of Chicago Law School.*

THE UNIVERSITY OF CHICAGO PRESS, CHICAGO 60637
The University of Chicago Press, Ltd., London
© 1949, 2013 by The University of Chicago
All rights reserved. Published 2013.
Printed in the United States of America

22 21 20 19 18 17 16 15 14 13   1 2 3 4 5

ISBN-13: 978-0-226-08972-0 (paper)
ISBN-13: 978-0-226-08986-7 (e-book)
DOI: 10.7208/chicago/9780226089867.001.0001

LIBRARY OF CONGRESS CATALOGING-IN-PUBLICATION DATA

Levi, Edward H. (Edward Hirsch), 1911–2000, author.
  An introduction to legal reasoning / Edward H. Levi ;
  with a foreword by Frederick Schauer.
    pages ; cm
  Includes bibliographical references.
  ISBN 978-0-226-08972-0 (paperback : alkaline paper) — ISBN 978-0-226-08986-7
(e-book) 1. Law—United States—Interpretation and construction. 2. Law—Meth-
odology. I. Schauer, Frederick F., writer of added commentary. II. Title.
  KF425.L48 2013
  340'.19—dc23

                                                         2013017817

Foreword

FREDERICK SCHAUER

Originally published in 1949, *An Introduction to Legal Reasoning*, by Edward H. Levi, a scholar who went on to become dean of the University of Chicago Law School, president of the University of Chicago, and attorney general of the United States, owns the rare distinction of being a central work in two different legal literatures. First, the book is an important manifestation of, and contribution to, Legal Realist thinking, stressing law's manipulability far more than its constraint, and focusing on the phenomenon by which the overwhelming majority of hard and litigated cases can be framed and argued in different ways depending on the needs of the client and the skills of the lawyer. And, second, Levi's book offers, through an extensive series of accessible examples from common-law, statutory, and constitutional decision making, a persuasive case for the importance of analogical reasoning in law, as well as an equally compelling demonstration of the many ways

Frederick Schauer is the David and Mary Harrison Distinguished Professor of Law at the University of Virginia. He is the author of *Thinking Like a Lawyer: A New Introduction to Legal Reasoning* (Harvard, 2009), *Profiles, Probabilities, and Stereotypes* (Harvard, 2003), and *Playing By the Rules: A Philosophical Examination of Rule-Based Decision-Making in Law and in Life* (Oxford, 1991), and is the editor of Karl N. Llewellyn's *The Theory of Rules* (Chicago, 2011).

in which effective lawyers and creative judges use examples and analogies to persuade others of the soundness of their claims.

These two aspects of Levi's book are of course related. It is Levi's view that analogical reasoning is the principal method by which lawyers argue their cases, and reasoning by analogy is thus, for him, the primary window into law's manipulability. If in most of the hard cases that wind up in court there are examples from, and analogies with, previous decisions that can be presented on either side, then it is less "the law" and more the skill of the lawyers and the proclivities of the judges that will determine the outcome. In this brief foreword I will offer a slightly more extensive preview of the nature and enduring importance of these two central themes in this still-valuable book.

I. LEVI AND LEGAL REALISM

That Levi and his book are best situated within American Legal Realism is not a controversial proposition. Even a brief scan of his footnotes will reveal a dominance of the major figures in the Realist tradition. Still, there does exist considerable disagreement about just what Legal Realism,[1] or American Legal Realism,[2] stands for.[3] Many of those disagreements, however, are ones that

---

[1] The capitalization is intentional and important. Legal Realism, as a school of thought about law, must be distinguished from various philosophical perspectives in metaethics and metaphysics that are also designated as "realist." In philosophy, realist positions are committed to the view that there is a reality that exists apart from human perception and human choice. But by emphasizing the role of the judge in making law and thus by questioning the very idea of judge-independent law, Legal Realism stands in stark contrast to most manifestations of philosophical realism.

[2] American Legal Realism is to be distinguished as well from the very different Scandinavian Realism of Alf Ross, Axel Hägerström, Karl Olivecrona, and Vilhelm Lundstedt, which is concerned with the ontological status of law and very little with legal reasoning and legal argument. *See* Gregory S. Alexander, *Comparing the Two Legal Realisms: American and Scandinavian*, 50 Am. J. Comp. L. 131 (2002).

[3] Thus there now exist newer and nonstandard understandings of American Legal Realism that see it as a challenge to law's alleged political and ideological neutrality, *see, e.g.*, Morton J. Horwitz, The Transformation of American Law, 1870–1960: The Crisis of

long postdate Levi's life and career. If we turn to the understanding of Realism that flourished in and shortly before Levi's time, and remains prominent still,[4] we can identify several important strands of the Realist perspective. One is the belief that judicial decision making and opinion writing are primarily a process of ex post justification, or, to put it less charitably, albeit by using a term that the Realists themselves employed, rationalization. From Jerome Frank[5] and Joseph Hutcheson[6] on, most of the Realists believed that judges did not initially consult the law in order then to reach a result on the basis of the facts that they or a jury had found, as the traditional or so-called formalist view would have it. Rather, they thought that judges first reached a result principally on nonlegal grounds, and only thereafter consulted the formal law in order to provide a legal justification or rationalization for the non-law-produced outcome.

Although the Realists agreed that neither formal law nor canonical legal doctrine played a major role in determining the outcomes of litigated cases, they nevertheless differed as to what actually produced outcomes in court. Some, like Frank, believed that judicial decisions were primarily the product of a range of personal characteristics of the judge reacting to the particular features of the litigants and their positions as well as to other

Legal Orthodoxy 169–212 (Harvard, 1992), as the forerunner of modern empirical legal studies, *see* Thomas J. Miles & Cass R. Sunstein, *The New Legal Realism*, 75 U. Chi. L. Rev. 831 (2008), or as the ancestor of the law and society movement, *see* Sally Engle Merry, *New Legal Realism and the Ethnography of Transnational Law*, 31 Law & Soc. Inq. 975 (2006). But Levi's own understanding of what made him a self-identified Realist was far removed from any of these perspectives.

⁴ *See* Brian Leiter, Naturalizing Jurisprudence: Essays on American Legal Realism and Naturalism in Legal Philosophy (Oxford, 2007); Frederick Schauer, Thinking Like a Lawyer: A New Introduction to Legal Reasoning 124–147 (Harvard, 2009); Frederick Schauer, *Editor's Introduction* to Karl N. Llewellyn, The Theory of Rules 1–28 (Chicago, 2011); Frederick Schauer, *Legal Realism Untamed*, 91 Texas L. Rev. 749 (2013).

⁵ Jerome Frank, Law and the Modern Mind (Brentano's, 1930).

⁶ Joseph C. Hutcheson Jr., *The Judgment Intuitive: The Role of the "Hunch" in Judicial Decision*, 14 Cornell L.Q. 274 (1929).

characteristics of the specific situation. Frank almost certainly did not attribute judicial outcomes to "what the judge had for breakfast," as the common caricature of Realism puts it, but he and a few other Realists did stress the personal and idiosyncratic reactions of judges to particular cases. Other Realists, however, Karl Llewellyn most prominently,[7] stressed the way in which judges reached what they thought was the best decision on policy grounds. And still others, including Llewellyn at times,[8] as well as Herman Oliphant,[9] Underhill Moore,[10] and others within mainstream Realism, saw judges reacting primarily to the facts and equities of the cases before them. This reaction might have been highly particularistic, with the judge trying to reach the best or most equitable outcome for the specific case. Or instead judges might see the facts of the cases as fitting within particular fact patterns or categories or "situation-types," albeit not the patterns or categories or types identified by formal legal doctrine.[11] So when the Realist Leon Green edited a then-prominent casebook on tort law,[12] he organized the cases according to what he believed were the genuine categories of decision—cases dealing with firearms, with surgical operations, and with trees and fences, for example—rather than the more abstract categories and doctrines of tort law, such as negligence, strict liability, causation, and foreseeability.

Levi and *An Introduction to Legal Reasoning* are best understood as falling within this last-described version of Legal Realism.

---

[7] *See* Karl N. Llewellyn, The Theory of Rules (Frederick Schauer ed., Chicago, 2011); Karl N. Llewellyn, The Common Law Tradition: Deciding Appeals (Little, Brown, 1960); William Twining, Karl Llewellyn and the Realist Movement (Cambridge, 2d ed., 2012).

[8] Karl N. Llewellyn, The Bramble Bush: Of Law and Its Study (Columbia, 1930); Karl N. Llewellyn, *Some Realism about Realism*, 44 Harv. L. Rev. 1222 (1931); Karl N. Llewellyn, *A Realistic Jurisprudence—The Next Step*, 30 Colum. L. Rev. 431 (1930).

[9] Herman Oliphant, *A Return to Stare Decisis*, 14 A.B.A.J. 71 (1928).

[10] *See* John Henry Schlegel, *American Legal Realism and Empirical Social Science: The Singular Case of Underhill Moore*, 29 Buff. L. Rev. 195 (1980).

[11] *See* Leiter, *supra* note 4.

[12] Leon Green, The Judicial Process in Tort Cases (West, 1931).

Levi said that the formal statement of a legal rule, just like the "meaning of a statute or of a constitution," is "window dressing."[13] "Particularly when a concept has broken down and reasoning by example is about to build another, textbook writers, well aware of the unreal aspect of old rules, will announce new ones, equally ambiguous and meaningless, forgetting that the legal process does not work with the rule but on a much lower level."[14]

This statement is slightly more extreme than the flavor that emerges from much of the rest of the book, but Levi's "much lower level" remains his key idea. Like most Realists, he understood judges and lawyers to be reacting primarily to the facts of particular cases and not to abstract legal rules. Indeed, like most of the Realists, he tended to collapse the distinction between the lawyer and the judge. Just as lawyers were concerned chiefly with pressing the goals of their clients, so too were judges, according to the Realists, concerned mainly with advancing a position they reached on those policy or equitable grounds that legal traditionalists would have considered as outside the law. Although Levi throughout the book offered instances of judges using examples and analogies to press for certain policy outcomes, even more did he see judges as decision makers who were primarily concerned to reach the best or most equitable result in the particular case, rather than thinking at any level of consciousness about which category in which to place those facts. So although Levi's description of the statement of a rule as "window dressing" is largely hyperbolic and misleading, even as to his own views, it does accurately capture his view that law operates at the level of particulars and not at the level of abstraction. If a judge's reaction to the particular facts of some controversy would produce what that judge believed to be a result inconsistent with the existing abstractions we call legal rules, the judge could, according to Levi, modify the rule in the circumstances of its application in

---

[13] Edward H. Levi, An Introduction to Legal Reasoning 9 (Chicago, 2013).
[14] *Id.*

order to accommodate the best result. And thus for Levi, like for other Realists, formal legal rules were best understood not as guides to judicial decision but more as revisable summaries of decisions reached in the past.[15] These rules might operate as useful heuristics or "rules of thumb" for the judge, but if the judge believed the right result (determined by some other and typically unwritten rule or principle) for some case was in tension with the indications of the previously understood rule, then it was that rule and not the best outcome that would be forced to give way.

As Levi himself implicitly acknowledged, his account is far more resonant with common-law adjudication than it is with the interpretation of precise statutory or constitutional language. But even with respect to statutory and constitutional interpretation, Levi also recognized what now goes by the name of the selection effect.[16] The basic idea is straightforward: Easy cases are rarely litigated, and that is primarily because when the law is clear the expected loser will rarely have an incentive to waste time and money and effort in the service of a losing cause. And if easy applications of the law are not litigated at all, or, if litigated, quickly settled and certainly not appealed, then the domain of litigated cases is disproportionately made up of hard cases—cases in which

---

[15] In criticizing the Realists, H. L. A. Hart accused them of ignoring the guiding and constraining dimension of rules, H. L. A. Hart, The Concept of Law 137–138 (Penelope A. Bulloch, Joseph Raz & Leslie Green eds., Oxford, 3d ed., 2012), but the mistake was Hart's and not the Realists'. The Realists well understood that rules could guide and constrain, but they believed that the rules that did so for judges were not necessarily the "paper rules," the rules set forth in formal and official legal sources. Thus we best understand Levi as believing that there are descriptive rules that usefully summarize previous decisions (something that Hart would not have denied), but that judges might modify those rules in the service of other unwritten rules or unwritten guides to the proper decision.

[16] One of the canonical modern sources is George L. Priest & Benjamin Klein, *The Selection of Disputes for Litigation*, 13 J. Legal Stud. 1 (1984). Useful summaries include Richard A. Posner, Economic Analysis of Law §21 (Little, Brown, 3d ed., 1986); Leandra Lederman, *Which Cases Go to Trial? An Empirical Study of Predictions of Failure to Settle*, 49 Case West. Res. L. Rev. 315 (1999); Frederick Schauer, *Judging in a Corner of the Law*, 61 S. Cal. L. Rev. 1717 (1988).

opposing parties with mutually exclusive views each believe they have a chance to prevail. Thus, although judges might in the abstract not favor the outcomes that would be produced by hard and crisp statutory or constitutional rules, the very hardness and crispness of those rules would typically prevent litigation in the first place, and the judges would never even have the opportunity to consider changing the rules. But sometimes a statute will not be hard and crisp—it will be vague, and thus a standard and not a rule in the contemporary terminology—and sometimes a case will exist on the edge of a seemingly crisp rule, as with H. L. A. Hart's well-known example of the question whether a bicycle is a "vehicle" for purposes of a rule prohibiting vehicles in the park. In these cases, Levi argued, correctly, that the application of the statute is sufficiently debatable, so that the distinction between common-law adjudication and statutory interpretation comes close to dissolving. Consider, for example, the recent United States Supreme Court case of *Lozman v. City of Riviera Beach, Florida.*[17] The question in the case was the propriety of admiralty jurisdiction, which turned out to depend on whether a houseboat was to be consider a "vessel" for purposes of the relevant statute.[18] Although there was indeed a statute, nothing in the statute answered the question about how best to characterize a houseboat, and thus the case and the arguments for the two sides turned out to be highly similar to the kinds of common arguments about characterization that Levi featured in the early parts of this book. Once the easy cases drop out of the equation, the distinctions

[17] 133 S. Ct. 735 (2013).

[18] The Supreme Court concluded, over a dissent, that the houseboat was not a vessel, largely because of its lack of a capacity for self-propulsion. Interestingly, a few years earlier, in a case called *Stewart v. Dutra Barge Co.*, 543 U.S. 481 (2005), the Court had ruled that a huge dredge called the *Super Scoop* was a vessel and not a piece of harbor machinery, largely because of the *Super Scoop*'s captain, crew, and (very limited) capacity for propulsion. It is clear that Levi, most obviously, and other Realists could have made much about the two cases, and about the reasons they were decided the way they were.

among common-law, statutory, and constitutional cases decrease dramatically. Recognizing this facet of litigation remains one of Levi's enduring contributions to how we understand legal argument and legal reasoning.

2. LEVI AND THE ROLE OF EXAMPLES

To their credit, neither Levi nor Llewellyn nor many of the other Realists believed that the right or just or equitable result in a particular case would simply jump out at the judge. This kind of outcome salience might occur in cases of manifest injustice, or in cases in which judges were likely to have strong moral or political or ideological views, but more commonly even what Llewellyn called the "fireside equities" of a case would be open to argument. This is where, for Levi, examples and analogies become so important. It is true that the constraint of precedent in the formal sense of a judge being bound to follow an identical previous decision even with which he or she disagrees is different from drawing an analogy to a nonidentical past case or decision.[19] Lawyers, however, are trained from the first day in law school to think that past decisions are important, and to believe that continuity with previous decisions is a valuable legal goal and an essential feature of legal argument. As a result, lawyers who seek to persuade judges of the rightness of their cause will draw an analogy with a previous decision in the hope of convincing the judge who agrees with that past decision that this case is of the same variety. Similarly, judges who want to persuade the audience for their opinions will treat past decisions in much the same way. And this preference of lawyers and judges for using previous decisions persists even when the decisions they use are not controlling precedents in the strict sense—that is, in the sense of being so close to the current case on the facts and questions presented that

---

[19] *See* Frederick Schauer, *Why Precedent in Law (and Elsewhere) Is Not Totally (or Even Substantially) about Analogy*, 3 Perspectives on Psychological Science 454 (2008).

anyone who acknowledges the constraints of precedent must be bound by such virtually identical precedents. Once we recognize that the selection effect serves to make most of the formal effects of precedent in this strict sense invisible, we can see that the overwhelming bulk of references to past cases in lawyers' briefs and judges' opinions are appeals to analogy rather than arguments from the constraining force of binding precedent.

Thus we can appreciate the value in Levi's focus on analogical reasoning as being central to lawyers' arguments in litigated cases, especially litigated cases that have a strong common-law flavor. And although several generations of cognitive scientists and philosophers have offered various formal and empirical accounts of analogical reasoning,[20] Levi's valuable approach is to offer a book that is full of illuminating examples of exactly this process. Or, to put it differently, this book uses examples to argue for the importance and nature of argument by example. Some of Levi's examples come from classic common-law areas such as torts and property and focus on such well-known exemplars of common-law reasoning as *MacPherson v. Buick*[21] and *Donoghue v. Stevenson.*[22] Other examples are drawn from cases in which the analogies are used to argue for one or another of competing but plausible interpretations of a statute or a constitutional provision; Levi's detailed discussion of the Supreme Court's interpretation of "commerce" is not only illuminating in its own right but highly timely in light of the recent Supreme Court decision on the Affordable Care Act of 2010.[23] But whether pure common-law

---

[20] Useful entries into this literature would include The Analogical Mind: Perspectives from Cognitive Science (Dedre Gentner, Keith J. Holyoak & Boris N. Kokinov eds., MIT, 2001); Keith J. Holyoak & Paul Thagard, Mental Leaps: Analogy in Creative Thought (MIT, 1995); Similarity and Analogical Reasoning (Stella Vosniadou & Andrew Ortony eds., Cambridge, 1989).

[21] III N.E. 1050 (N.Y. 1916).

[22] [1932] A.C. 562.

[23] National Federation of Independent Businesses v. Sebelius, 132 S. Ct. 2566 (2012).

decisions, or decisions interpreting a statute or a constitutional provision, all of Levi's examples are essentially and intentionally examples of analogical argument.

Levi's focus on analogical argument meshes nicely with his Legal Realist worldview. Rarely in this book do we find Levi declaring that some judicial decision was right or wrong. Rather, he implicitly argued that most judicial decisions can be located within a domain of plausibility, with the persuasiveness of the analogy being key to understanding why courts accept some plausible outcomes and reject others. And, once one of these plausible outcomes has been accepted, the case in which it has been accepted can then provide the analogical platform—the source analogue, in today's technical terminology—for future analogical arguments and counterarguments. And so it goes continuously, with the ability of a lawyer to use more or less persuasive analogies in an effort to get a court to decide a case in his or her client's favor and thus to move the law in one direction rather than another.

The role of the lawyer in all of this should not be underestimated. Karl Llewellyn, perhaps more than any other Realist, understood the role of advocacy skill in producing judicial outcomes, and Levi mostly followed in Llewellyn's path. Analogies and examples do not just leap into the judge's consciousness. Rather, the potential and competing analogies are presented by opposing counsel, and, for Levi and for Llewellyn and for others, the skill of the advocate in locating the right analogy and presenting it persuasively is at least as important as anything inherent in one analogy rather than another in determining which analogy will prevail.

3. THE STATUS OF LEVI'S PICTURE

Levi's Legal Realism and his almost exclusive focus on analogical reasoning in law were not without controversy when he wrote *An Introduction to Legal Reasoning* in 1949, nor are they today. With respect to Realism, even the Realists themselves acknowledged that their claims were irreducibly empirical, and thus there persists the question whether Levi's picture of legal decision making is in fact accurate. Are legal outcomes as beholden to the result of the clash of analogies as Levi supposed, or might formal legal rules and published precedents and widely accepted legal doctrines play a greater causal role in producing outcomes than Levi and most other Realists imagined?[24] And, from the other direction, is Levi Realist enough? Are there better and worse examples and analogies, as Levi at times seems to suggest, or do judges choose between or among the analogies offered by counsel not on the basis of which analogies resonate and which do not, but rather on the basis of the judge's own policy-based or equity-based or personality-based outcome preferences, with the analogies themselves serving the same kind of rationalizing role that the Realists thought was the case with respect to formal rules and doctrines?

Even Levi's account of analogical reasoning itself has been subject to challenge. Prominent judges such as Richard Posner[25] and academics such as Larry Alexander[26] and Peter Westen[27] have questioned whether analogical reasoning is genuinely distinct, or is instead a form of rule-based reasoning with disguised premises, where descriptions of reasoning by example and reasoning by analogy are themselves attempts to mask a process by which judges are simply making law but refusing to admit it. Of course Levi

---

[24] Prominent contemporary arguments to this effect include Charles Fried, Order and Law: Arguing the Reagan Revolution—A Firsthand Account 60–67 (Simon & Schuster, 1991); Randy E. Barnett, *The Sound of Silence: Default Rules and Constitutional Consent*, 78 Va. L. Rev. 821, 909 (1992); James Gordley, *Legal Reasoning: An Introduction*, 72 Calif. L. Rev. 138 (1984).

[25] Richard A. Posner, *Reasoning by Analogy*, 91 Cornell L. Rev. 761 (2006).

[26] Larry Alexander, *The Banality of Legal Reasoning*, 73 Notre Dame L. Rev. 517 (1998).

[27] Peter Westen, *On "Confusing Ideas,"* 91 Yale L.J. 1153 (1982).

does have other legal academics[28] and most cognitive scientists[29] on his side, many of whom believe that the process of reasoning from example to example without the intervention of a mediating abstraction is an accurate portrayal of much of human, and, therefore, legal and judicial, reasoning.

This is not the occasion to even begin to resolve the soundness of Levi's position, whether on Legal Realism or on reasoning by analogy, against his challengers. But there can be little doubt that both Legal Realism and the defense of analogical reasoning in law are enduring, important, and at the very least partially correct accounts of American legal advocacy and American judicial decision making. Although some of Levi's examples may be dated, many are not, and the positions he advances certainly are not. *An Introduction to Legal Reasoning* was, when published, an important contribution to the distinctively American view of legal argument, legal reasoning, legal decision making, and legal thought. It remains so to this day, and by no means solely for historical reasons.

[28] *See* Kent Greenawalt, Statutory and Common Law Interpretation 217–44 (Oxford, 2012); Lloyd L. Weinreb, Legal Reason: The Use of Analogy in Legal Argument (Cambridge, 2005); Scott Brewer, *Exemplary Reasoning: Semantics, Pragmatics, and the Rational Force of Legal Argument by Analogy*, 109 Harv. L. Rev. 923 (1996); Barbara A. Spellman, *Judges, Expertise, and Analogy, in* The Psychology of Judicial Decision Making 146 (David Klein & Gregory Mitchell eds., Oxford, 2010); Cass R. Sunstein, *On Analogical Reasoning*, 106 Harv. L. Rev. 741 (1993).

[29] *See supra* note 20.

Preface

This preface provides the opportunity to make only brief reference to certain recent jurisprudential discussions. The first of these discussions concerns the possible application of the analysis developed in the essay to the trial court level. The examples used in the essay are mostly of cases which have reached the appellate stage and which therefore have been exposed to the full range of the disciplined process. And so it can be said, as Judge Frank wrote in his *Courts on Trial*,[1] that the approach slights the crucial fact-finding stage of the trial court, the "pain and anguish of giving birth to the facts which are compared with those in earlier cases," and the many factors, including such subjective elements as the sartorial appearance of a witness or a party, which may have an impact upon the trier of fact. Judge Frank stressed the discretionary element involved in fact categorization at the trial level. Dean O'Meara, on the other hand, while finding much of the fruitfulness of the natural law approach in the creative nature of the judge's role, suggests the essay overemphasizes the leeway available to law, because in many cases, particularly those which do not get to the appellate level or do not get into court at all, "a well established principle, expressive of the earlier decisions, is clearly dispositive of the controversy."[2]

[1] Frank, Courts on Trial, 321, 325 (1949).

[2] O'Meara, Natural Law and Everyday Law, 5 Natural L. Forum 83, 87 (1960).

Judge Frank was writing about the uncertainty of facts at the trial level; Dean O'Meara, if I understand him correctly, is arguing for the greater certainty of law at that stage.

I believe the studies now going forward at the University of Chicago Law School on the jury system and on arbitration[3] will provide insights on the impact of some subjective factors or at least on the frequency with which a similar set of circumstances may be seen in one way or another by fact-finders who are decision-makers. But I hope the process described in this essay is recognizable as dealing just as much with fact determination or categorization as with rule-making. One can accept the persuasiveness of the legal concept as a rule of thumb, and particularly so at the trial or at an earlier stage, and yet marvel at the numerous possibilities, more open at the trial than at the appellate level, to shape the case by an interpretation of the facts in light of a re-examination of the law.

Second, Professor Montrose[4] and Mr. Cross[5] have made explicit, within the analytical framework of reasoning by example, the view of many English judges, particularly during the last decade, that modern English judicial practice restricts the freedom of the English judge to disregard the reasoning advanced by earlier courts. As Mr. Cross has written, "The effect of the rigid English doctrine of precedent is that our judges frequently do have to try to see the law through the eyes of their predecessors." There are, of course, styles in

[3] Kalven, The Jury, the Law and the Personal Injury Damage Award, 19 Ohio St. L. J. 158 (1958); Mentschikoff, Commercial Arbitration, 61 Col. L. Rev. 846 (1961).

[4] Montrose, Return to Austin's College, 10, 11 (1960).

[5] Cross, Precedent in English Law, 207 (1961); cf. Oxford Essays in Jurisprudence, 148, 176 (Ed. by Guest, 1961) (Simpson, The Ratio Decidendi of a Case and the Doctrine of Binding Precedent, and Guest, Logic in the Law); Wasserstrom, The Judicial Decision, 50 (1961); Davis, The Future of Judge-made Public Law in England: A Problem of Practical Jurisprudence, 61 Col. L. Rev. 201 (1961).

opinion writing and in the enthusiasm with which judges approach the problem of re-examining the consequences and purposes of laws.[6] With some temerity I question whether the actual practice of English and American judges is so divergent. I do not think that the duty of the American judge to view the law as a fairly consistent whole, seeing the law through his own eyes, and not through the eyes of his predecessor, leads to a dominant pattern of complete rejection of the reasoning of earlier courts, or to the making of distinctions when there is no reasonable ground for doing so. Granted that *Donoghue v. Stevenson* was on the hearing of a Scots appeal, I wonder whether in practice the English judge is limited in his vision to the views of a prior court when it would be reasonable to distinguish the situations. Perhaps, in comparing the two systems, a field of case law alone is often contrasted with statutory interpretation, where, to quote Lord Evershed, the question is whether "the judiciary should assume the function of law-makers in spite of, or in conflict with, the enacted law."[7] It is indeed in the field of statutory interpretation that the suggestion of this essay is that the subsequent judge is also fettered under the American system, when no constitutional matter is involved. The 1953 decision of the United States Supreme Court holding the antitrust laws inapplicable to baseball is a fascinating example of this.[8]

Third, this essay in the constitutional area stresses both shifts in doctrine and the persuasion of similar situations. The persuasion of similar situations is itself a reflection of the principle of equality and of the impact of social setting; it makes the application of law, in a proper sense, result-oriented. Questions concerning the duty of a court to structure doc-

[6] Llewellyn, The Common Law Tradition (1960).

[7] Evershed, The Judicial Process in Twentieth Century England, 61 Col. L. Rev. 761 (1961).

[8] Toolson v. New York Yankees, 346 U.S. 356 (1953).

trine and to anticipate the developments of a moving classification system raise central issues with respect to legal reasoning. In this connection, reference is made to Professor Wechsler's call, and the resulting discussion, for the reasoned use, in the field of constitutional interpretation, of neutral principles which transcend the immediate result in the particular case.[9]

[9] Wechsler, Principles, Politics, and Fundamental Law, 3 (1961); Hart, Foreword: The Time Chart of the Justices, 73 Harv. L. Rev. 84 (1959); Arnold, Professor Hart's Theology, 73 Harv. L. Rev. 1298 (1960); Griswold: Of Time and Attitudes—Professor Hart and Judge Arnold, 74 Harv. L. Rev. 81 (1960).

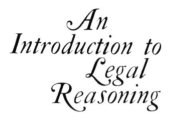

An
Introduction to
Legal
Reasoning

I

This is an attempt to describe generally the process of legal reasoning in the field of case law and in the interpretation of statutes and of the Constitution. It is important that the mechanism of legal reasoning should not be concealed by its pretense. The pretense is that the law is a system of known rules applied by a judge; the pretense has long been under attack.[1] In an important sense legal rules are never clear, and, if a rule had to be clear before it could be imposed, society would be impossible. The mechanism accepts the differences of view and ambiguities of words. It provides for the participation of the community in resolving the ambiguity by providing a forum for the discussion of policy in the gap of ambiguity. On serious controversial questions, it makes it possible to take the first step in the direction of what otherwise would be forbidden ends. The mechanism is indispensable to peace in a community.

The basic pattern of legal reasoning is reasoning by example.[2] It is reasoning from case to case. It is a three-step process

[1] The controlling book is Frank, Law and the Modern Mind (1936).

[2] "Clearly then to argue by example is neither like reasoning from part to whole, nor like reasoning from whole to part, but rather reasoning from part to part, when both particulars are subordinate to the same term and one of them is known. It differs from induction, because induction starting from all the particular cases proves . . . that the major term belongs to the middle

described by the doctrine of precedent in which a proposition descriptive of the first case is made into a rule of law and then applied to a next similar situation. The steps are these: similarity is seen between cases; next the rule of law inherent in the first case is announced; then the rule of law is made applicable to the second case. This is a method of reasoning necessary for the law, but it has characteristics which under other circumstances might be considered imperfections.

These characteristics become evident if the legal process is approached as though it were a method of applying general rules of law to diverse facts—in short, as though the doctrine of precedent meant that general rules, once properly determined, remained unchanged, and then were applied, albeit imperfectly, in later cases. If this were the doctrine, it would be disturbing to find that the rules change from case to case and are remade with each case. Yet this change in the rules is the indispensable dynamic quality of law. It occurs because the scope of a rule of law, and therefore its meaning, depends upon a determination of what facts will be considered similar to those present when the rule was first announced. The finding of similarity or difference is the key step in the legal process.

The determination of similarity or difference is the function of each judge. Where case law is considered, and there is no statute, he is not bound by the statement of the rule of law made by the prior judge even in the controlling case. The statement is mere dictum, and this means that the judge in the present case may find irrelevant the existence or absence of facts which prior judges thought important.[3] It is not what the

---

and does not apply the syllogistic conclusion to the minor term, whereas argument by example does make this application and does not draw its proof from all the particular cases." Aristotle, Analytica Priora 69a (McKeon ed., 1941).

[3] But cf. Goodhart, Determining the Ratio Decidendi of a Case, 40 Yale L. J. 161 (1930).

prior judge intended that is of any importance; rather it is what the present judge, attempting to see the law as a fairly consistent whole, thinks should be the determining classification. In arriving at his result he will ignore what the past thought important; he will emphasize facts which prior judges would have thought made no difference. It is not alone that he could not see the law through the eyes of another, for he could at least try to do so. It is rather that the doctrine of dictum forces him to make his own decision.[4]

Thus it cannot be said that the legal process is the application of known rules to diverse facts. Yet it is a system of rules; the rules are discovered in the process of determining similarity or difference. But if attention is directed toward the finding of similarity or difference, other peculiarities appear. The problem for the law is: When will it be just to treat different cases as though they were the same? A working legal system must therefore be willing to pick out key similarities and to reason from them to the justice of applying a common classification. The existence of some facts in common brings into play the general rule. If this is really reasoning, then by common standards, thought of in terms of closed systems, it is imperfect unless some overall rule has announced that this common and ascertainable similarity is to be decisive. But no such fixed prior rule exists. It could be suggested that reasoning is not involved at all; that is, that no new insight is arrived at through a comparison of cases. But reasoning appears to be involved; the conclusion is arrived at through a process and was not immediately apparent. It seems better to say there is reasoning, but it is imperfect.[5]

Therefore it appears that the kind of reasoning involved in the legal process is one in which the classification changes as the classification is made. The rules change as the rules are

---

[4] Cf. Mead, The Philosophy of the Act 81, 92–102 (1938).

[5] The logical fallacy is the fallacy of the undistributed middle or the fallacy of assuming the antecedent is true because the consequent has been affirmed.

applied. More important, the rules arise out of a process which, while comparing fact situations, creates the rules and then applies them. But this kind of reasoning is open to the charge that it is classifying things as equal when they are somewhat different, justifying the classification by rules made up as the reasoning or classification proceeds. In a sense all reasoning is of this type,[6] but there is an additional requirement which compels the legal process to be this way. Not only do new situations arise, but in addition peoples' wants change. The categories used in the legal process must be left ambiguous in order to permit the infusion of new ideas. And this is true even where legislation or a constitution is involved. The words used by the legislature or the constitutional convention must come to have new meanings. Furthermore, agreement on any other basis would be impossible. In this manner the laws come to express the ideas of the community and even when written in general terms, in statute or constitution, are molded for the specific case.

But attention must be paid to the process. A controversy as to whether the law is certain, unchanging, and expressed in rules, or uncertain, changing, and only a technique for deciding specific cases misses the point. It is both. Nor is it helpful to dispose of the process as a wonderful mystery possibly reflecting a higher law, by which the law can remain the same and yet change. The law forum is the most explicit demonstration of the mechanism required for a moving classification system. The folklore of law may choose to ignore the imperfections in legal reasoning,[7] but the law forum itself has taken care of them.

[6] Dewey, Logic, The Theory of Inquiry, Ch. 6 (1938); cf. Pareto, The Mind and Society § 894 (1935); Arnold, The Folklore of Capitalism, Ch. 7 (1937).

[7] "That the law can be obeyed even when it grows is often more than the legal profession itself can grasp." Cohen and Nagel, An Introduction to Logic and Scientific Method 371 (1934); see Stone, The Province and Function of Law 140–206 (1946).

What does the law forum require? It requires the presentation of competing examples. The forum protects the parties and the community by making sure that the competing analogies are before the court. The rule which will be created arises out of a process in which if different things are to be treated as similar, at least the differences have been urged.[8] In this sense the parties as well as the court participate in the law-making. In this sense, also, lawyers represent more than the litigants.

Reasoning by example in the law is a key to many things. It indicates in part the hold which the law process has over the litigants. They have participated in the law-making. They are bound by something they helped to make. Moreover, the examples or analogies urged by the parties bring into the law the common ideas of the society. The ideas have their day in court, and they will have their day again. This is what makes the hearing fair, rather than any idea that the judge is completely impartial, for of course he cannot be completely so. Moreover, the hearing in a sense compels at least vicarious participation by all the citizens, for the rule which is made, even though ambiguous, will be law as to them.

Reasoning by example shows the decisive role which the common ideas of the society and the distinctions made by experts can have in shaping the law. The movement of common or expert concepts into the law may be followed. The concept is suggested in arguing difference or similarity in a brief, but it wins no approval from the court. The idea achieves standing in the society. It is suggested again to a court. The court this time reinterprets the prior case and in doing so adopts the rejected idea. In subsequent cases, the idea is given further

---

[8] The reasoning may take this form: A falls more appropriately in B than in C. It does so because A is more like D which is of B than it is like E which is of C. Since A is in B and B is in G (legal concept), then A is in G. But perhaps C is in G also. If so, then B is in a decisively different segment of G, because B is like H which is in G and has a different result from C.

definition and is tied to other ideas which have been accepted by courts. It is now no longer the idea which was commonly held in the society. It becomes modified in subsequent cases. Ideas first rejected but which gradually have won acceptance now push what has become a legal category out of the system or convert it into something which may be its opposite. The process is one in which the ideas of the community and of the social sciences, whether correct or not, as they win acceptance in the community, control legal decisions. Erroneous ideas, of course, have played an enormous part in shaping the law. An idea, adopted by a court, is in a superior position to influence conduct and opinion in the community; judges, after all, are rulers. And the adoption of an idea by a court reflects the power structure in the community. But reasoning by example will operate to change the idea after it has been adopted.

Moreover, reasoning by example brings into focus important similarity and difference in the interpretation of case law, statutes, and the constitution of a nation. There is a striking similarity. It is only folklore which holds that a statute if clearly written can be completely unambiguous and applied as intended to a specific case. Fortunately or otherwise, ambiguity is inevitable in both statute and constitution as well as with case law. Hence reasoning by example operates with all three. But there are important differences. What a court says is dictum, but what a legislature says is a statute. The reference of the reasoning changes. Interpretation of intention when dealing with a statute is the way of describing the attempt to compare cases on the basis of the standard thought to be common at the time the legislation was passed. While this is the attempt, it may not initially accomplish any different result than if the standard of the judge had been explicitly used. Nevertheless, the remarks of the judge are directed toward describing a category set up by the legislature. These remarks are different from ordinary dicta. They set the course of the statute, and later reasoning in subsequent cases is tied to them. As a consequence, courts are less free in applying a statute than in dealing with case law. The current rationale for this is the notion that the legislature has acquiesced by legislative silence in the prior, even though erroneous, interpretation of the court. But the change in reasoning where legislation is concerned seems an inevitable consequence of the division of function between court and legislature, and, paradoxically, a recognition also of the impossibility of determining legislative intent. The impairment of a court's freedom in interpreting legislation is reflected in frequent appeals to the constitution as a necessary justification for overruling cases even though these cases are thought to have interpreted the legislation erroneously.

Under the United States experience, contrary to what has sometimes been believed when a written constitution of a nation is involved, the court has greater freedom than it has with the application of a statute or case law. In case law, when a judge determines what the controlling similarity between the present and prior case is, the case is decided. The judge does not feel free to ignore the results of a great number of cases which he cannot explain under a remade rule. And in interpreting legislation, when the prior interpretation, even though erroneous, is determined after a comparison of facts to cover the case, the case is decided. But this is not true with a constitution. The constitution sets up the conflicting ideals of the community in certain ambiguous categories.[9] These categories bring along with them satellite concepts covering the areas of ambiguity. It is with a set of these satellite concepts that reasoning by example must work. But no satellite concept, no matter how well developed, can prevent the court from shifting its course, not only by realigning cases which impose cer-

[9] Compare Myrdal, An American Dilemma, Ch. 1 (1944); Dicey, Law of the Constitution 126, 146 (9th ed., 1939).

tain restrictions, but by going beyond realignment back to the over-all ambiguous category written into the document. The constitution, in other words, permits the court to be inconsistent. The freedom is concealed either as a search for the intention of the framers or as a proper understanding of a living instrument, and sometimes as both. But this does not mean that reasoning by example has any less validity in this field.

II

It may be objected that this analysis of legal reasoning places too much emphasis on the comparison of cases and too little on the legal concepts which are created. It is true that similarity is seen in terms of a word, and inability to find a ready word to express similarity or difference may prevent change in the law. The words which have been found in the past are much spoken of, have acquired a dignity of their own, and to a considerable measure control results. As Judge Cardozo suggested in speaking of metaphors, the word starts out to free thought and ends by enslaving it.[10] The movement of concepts into and out of the law makes the point. If the society has begun to see certain significant similarities or differences, the comparison emerges with a word. When the word is finally accepted, it becomes a legal concept. Its meaning continues to change. But the comparison is not only between the instances which have been included under it and the actual case at hand, but also in terms of hypothetical instances which the word by itself suggests. Thus the connotation of the word for a time has a limiting influence—so much so that the reasoning may even appear to be simply deductive.

But it is not simply deductive. In the long run a circular motion can be seen. The first stage is the creation of the legal concept which is built up as cases are compared. The period is one in which the court fumbles for a phrase. Several phrases

[10] Berkey v. Third Ave. Ry. Co., 244 N.Y. 84, 94, 155 N.E. 58, 61 (1926).

may be tried out; the misuse or misunderstanding of words it-self may have an effect. The concept sounds like another, and the jump to the second is made. The second stage is the period when the concept is more or less fixed, although reasoning by example continues to classify items inside and out of the con-cept. The third stage is the breakdown of the concept, as rea-soning by example has moved so far ahead as to make it clear that the suggestive influence of the word is no longer desired.

The process is likely to make judges and lawyers uncom-fortable. It runs contrary to the pretense of the system. It seems inevitable, therefore, that as matters of kind vanish into matters of degree and then entirely new meanings turn up, there will be the attempt to escape to some overall rule which can be said to have always operated and which will make the reasoning look deductive. The rule will be useless. It will have to operate on a level where it has no meaning.[11] Even when lip service is paid to it, care will be taken to say that it may be too wide or too narrow but that nevertheless it is a good rule. The statement of the rule is roughly analogous to the appeal to the meaning of a statute or of a constitution, but it has less of a function to perform. It is window dressing. Yet it can be very misleading. Particularly when a concept has broken down and reasoning by example is about to build another, textbook writers, well aware of the unreal aspect of old rules, will announce new ones, equally ambiguous and meaningless, forgetting that the legal process does not work with the rule but on a much lower level.

The movement of legal concepts in case law has frequently been shown by pointing to the breakdown of the so-called "inherently dangerous" rule.[12] It is easy to do this because the

---

[11] See 3 Mill, A System of Logic, Ch. 1, § 2 (1887).

[12] The concept has been used for the precise demonstration intended here: Radin, Case Law and Stare Decisis: Concerning Prajudizienrecht in Amerika, 33 Col. L. Rev. 199 (1933); Llewellyn, The Status of the Rule of Judicial Precedent, 14 U. of Cin. L. Rev. 208 (1940); cf. Pound, What of Stare Decisis? 10 Fordham L. Rev. 1 (1941). In connection with the general problem, see

opinion in *MacPherson v. Buick Motor Co.*[13] is the work of a judge acutely conscious of the legal process and articulate about it. But *MacPherson v. Buick* was only a part of a cyclical movement in which differences and similarities first rejected are then adopted and later cast aside. The description of the movement can serve as an example of case law. Roughly the problem has become: the potential liability of a seller of an article which causes injury to a person who did not buy the article from the seller. In recent times the three phases in the movement of the concepts used in handling this problem can be traced.

The first of these begins in 1816 and carries us to 1851. It begins with a loaded gun and ends with an exploding lamp. The loaded gun brought liability to its owner in the case of *Dixon v. Bell.*[14] He had sent his thirteen- or fourteen-year-old servant girl to get the gun; in playing with the gun she had shot it off into the face of the plaintiff's son, who lost his right eye and two teeth. In holding that the plaintiff might recover, Lord Ellenborough attempted no classification of dangerous articles. He was content to describe the gun "as by this want of care . . . left in a state capable of doing mischief."[15] Thus the pattern begins with commodities mischievous through want of care.

The pattern becomes complicated in 1837 in the case of

---

also Fuller, Reason and Fiat in Case Law, 59 Harv. L. Rev. 376 (1946); Llewellyn, The Rule of Law in Our Case Law of Contract, 47 Yale L. J. 1243 (1938); Llewellyn, On Our Case Law of Contract: Offer and Acceptance, I, 48 Yale L. J. 1 (1938); Lobingier, Precedent in Past and Present Legal Systems, 44 Mich. L. Rev. 955 (1946); Rheinstein, The Place of Wrong: A Study in the Method of Case Law, 19 Tulane L. Rev. 4 (1944); cf. Republic of Mexico v. Hoffman, 324 U.S. 30 (1945).

[13] 217 N.Y. 382, 111 N.E. 1050 (1916); see Parker, Attorneys at Law, Ch. 8 (1942).

[14] 5 Maule & Selwyn 198 (1816).

[15] Ibid., at 199.

Langridge v. Levy,[16] where a plaintiff complained that the defendant had sold his father a defective gun for the use of himself and his sons. The gun had blown up in the plaintiff's hand. The court allowed recovery, apparently on the theory that the seller had falsely declared that the gun was safe when he knew it was defective and had sold the gun to the father knowing it was to be used by the plaintiff. It was therefore both a case of fraud and, in some sense, one of direct dealing between the seller and the plaintiff. The example used by the court was the case of a direct sale to the plaintiff, or where the instrument had been "placed in the hands of a third person for the purpose of being delivered to and then used by the plaintiff."[17] The direct dealing point is also emphasized by the statement of one of the judges during the argument to the effect that it would have helped the plaintiff's case if he had alleged that his father "was an unconscious agent in the transaction" because "the act of an unconscious agent is the act of the party who sets him in motion."[18]

In the argument of *Langridge v. Levy*, counsel for the defendant had pointed to a distinction between things "immediately dangerous or mischievous by the act of the defendant" and "such as may become so by some further act to be done to it."[19] They had urged what might be considered the pattern suggested by *Dixon v. Bell*. But the court rejected the use of any such distinction, although it remarked in passing that the gun was not "of itself dangerous, but . . . requires an act to be done, that is to be loaded, in order to make it so." It

[16] 2 Meeson & Welsby 519 (1837).

[17] Ibid., at 531.   [18] Alderson, B., ibid., at 525.

[19] Ibid., at 528; note also the hypothetical case set forth by counsel for the plaintiff in Langridge v. Levy reported in 6 L.J. (N.S.) Ex. 137, 138 (1837). "A case might be put of a wrong medicine sent from a chemist, which is received by a person, and placed by him in a cupboard, and afterwards taken by a third person, who, in consequence receives an injury; can it be said that he has no remedy against the chemist?"

rejected not only the distinction but any category of dangerous articles, because it "should pause before we made a precedent by our decision which would be an authority for an action against the vendors, even of such instruments and articles
as are dangerous in themselves, at the suit of *any person*
whomsoever into whose hands they might happen to pass and
who should be injured thereby."[20]

Nevertheless the category of dangerous articles and the distinction between things of a dangerous nature and those which
become so if improperly constructed (which need not be the
same as requiring a further act to be done to make it dangerous) were again urged before the court five years later in
Winterbottom v. Wright.[21] The court refused to permit a
coachman to recover against the defendant who had provided
a defective coach under contract with the Postmaster General. The plaintiff had been driving the coach from Hartford
to Holyhead when it broke down due to some latent defect;
the plaintiff was thrown from his seat and lamed for life. He
could not recover because to extend liability this far would
lead to "absurd and outrageous consequences." The court refused to discuss whether the defective coach was a weapon of
a dangerous nature, even though defendant's counsel seemed
to be willing to acknowledge the existence of a special rule of
liability for that category. And as for the application of *Langridge v. Levy*, in that case there was a "distinct fraud" and the
plaintiff "was really and substantially the party contracting."
The court refused to find similarity under the fraud concept
in the fact that the defendant had sold a coach as safe when he
did not know it to be in good condition, or under the direct
dealing concept in *Langridge v. Levy* in that "there was nothing to show that the defendant was aware even of the existence of the particular son who was injured" whereas here the

[20] Ibid., at 530.
[21] 10 Meeson & Welsby 109 (1842).

coach "was necessarily to be driven by a coachman."[22] The further argument that the plaintiff had no opportunity of seeing that the coach was sound and secure was insufficient to bring liability.

But in 1851, in *Longmeid v. Holliday*,[23] the concept of things dangerous in themselves, twice urged before the court and rejected, finally won out. Longmeid had bought a lamp for the use of himself and his wife from Holliday, the defendant storekeeper, who called the lamp "Holliday's Patent Lamp" and had it put together by other persons from parts which he had purchased. When Eliza Longmeid, the wife and plaintiff, tried to light the lamp, it exploded; the naphtha ran over her and scorched and burned her. She was not permitted to collect from the storekeeper. It had not been shown that the defendant knew the lamp was unfit and warranted it to be sound. And the lamp was not in its nature dangerous. In discussing those cases where a third person, not a party to a contract, might recover damages, the court said:

And it may be the same when any one delivers to another without notice an instrument in its nature dangerous, or under particular circumstances, as a loaded gun which he himself loaded, and that other person to whom it is delivered is injured thereby, or if he places it in a situation easily accessible to a third person, who sustains damage from it. A very strong case to that effect is *Dixon v. Bell*. But it would be going much too far to say that so much care is required in the ordinary intercourse of life between one individual and another, that, if a machine not in its nature dangerous,—a carriage for instance,—but which might become so by a latent defect entirely unknown, although discoverable by the exercise of ordinary care, should be lent or given by one person, even by the person who manufactured it, to another, the former should be answerable to the latter for a subesquent damage accruing by the use of it.[24]

22 Ibid., at 112.

23 155 Eng. Rep. 752 (1851).

24 Ibid., at 755. The opinion was by Parke, B.

Thus the doctrine of the distinction between things in their nature dangerous and those which become so by an unknown latent defect is announced as a way of explaining the difference between a loaded gun (which under the rule, however, is explained as a particular circumstance) and a defective lamp. As applied in the case, the doctrine describes the classification of the lamp as dangerous only through a latent defect and results in no liability. But a court could have found as much direct dealing in the purchase of a lamp for the use of the purchaser and his wife as in the case of the purchase of a gun for the use of the purchaser and his sons. Under the rule as stated a carriage is not in its nature dangerous.

The second phase of the development of the doctrine of dangerous articles is the period during which the rule as announced in the *Longmeid* case is applied. The phase begins with mislabeled poison and ends with a defective automobile. During this time also there is the inevitable attempt to soar above the cases and to find some great overall rule which can classify the cases as though the pattern were really not a changing one.

It was the purchase of belladonna, erroneously marked as extract of dandelion, which, in *Thomas v. Winchester*[25] in 1852, produced the first application and restatement of the rule announced in the *Longmeid* case. The poison had been bought at the store of Dr. Foord, but it had been put into its jar and incorrectly labeled in the shop of the defendant Winchester—probably through the negligence of his employee. Mrs. Thomas, who used what she thought was extract of dandelion, reacted by having "coldness of the surface and extremities, feebleness of circulation, spasms of the muscles, giddiness of the head, dilatation of the pupils of the eye and derangement of mind." She was allowed to recover against Winchester. The defendant's negligence had "put human life

[25] 6 N.Y. 397 (1852).

in imminent danger." No such imminent danger has existed in the *Winterbottom* case, the Court explained. This was more like the case of the loaded gun in *Dixon v. Bell*. The imminent danger category would not include a defective wagon but it did include poison.

Looking back, one might say today that the category of things by their nature dangerous or imminently dangerous soon came to include a defective hair wash. At least in *George v. Skivington*[26] in 1869, a chemist who compounded a secret hair wash was liable to the wife of the purchaser for injuries caused by the wash. But the court went about its business without explicit regard for the imminently dangerous category. It thought that the imperfect hair wash was like the imperfect gun in the *Langridge* case. It chose to ignore the emphasis in the *Langridge* case on the purported fact that the seller there knew the gun was defective and lied. It said, "substitute the word 'negligence' for fraud and the analogy between *Langridge v. Levy* and this case is complete." And as for the case of the defective lamp where there was no liability, that was different because negligence had not been found. In constructing a pattern for the cases, it appears that loaded guns, defective guns, poison, and now hair wash were in the imminently dangerous category. Defective wagons and lamps were outside.

The next year it became known that a defective balance wheel for a circular saw was not imminently dangerous. The New York court stated: "Poison is a dangerous subject. Gunpowder is the same. A torpedo is a dangerous instrument, as is a spring gun, a loaded rifle or the like. . . . Not so, however, an iron wheel, a few feet in diameter and a few inches in thickness although one part may be weaker than another. If the article is abused by too long use, or by applying too much weight or speed, an injury may occur, as it may from an ordi-

[26] 5 L.R. Ex. 1 (1869).

nary carriage wheel, a wagon axle, or the common chair in which we sit."[27] While applying the imminently dangerous category to defeat liability, the New York court took occasion to give a somewhat new emphasis to *Thomas v. Winchester.* It found that "the decision in *Thomas v. Winchester* was based upon the idea that the negligent sale of poisons is both at common law and by statute an indictable offense." And certainly that could be argued. At any rate, three years later the New York court said its opinion in the balance-wheel case showed that *Thomas v. Winchester* would not result in liability in a case where a boiler blew up.[28] But the imminently dangerous category received a new member in 1882 when the builder of a ninety-foot scaffold to be used in painting the dome of the courthouse was held liable to the estate of an employee-painter who was killed when the ledger gave way.[29] Yet if a defective scaffold was in, the court followed tradition in announcing that a defective carriage would be out.

In England a defective scaffold was also put in the category. The plaintiff in *Heaven v. Pender*[30] was a ship painter who was injured, while engaged in his work, due to the breaking of defective ropes which held his support outside the ship. He was allowed to recover against the dock owner who had supplied the support and ropes. But the majority of the judges decided the case on the rather narrow point that the necessary workmen were in effect invited by the dock owner to use the dock and appliances. That could have been the explanation also for the American scaffold case. The most noteworthy feature of *Heaven v. Pender*, however, was the flight of one of the judges, Lord Esher, at that time Brett, to-

---

[27] Loop v. Litchfield, 42 N.Y. 351, 359 (1870).

[28] Losee v. Clute, 51 N.Y. 494 (1873).

[29] Devlin v. Smith, 89 N.Y. 470 (1882).

[30] 11 L.R. Q.B. 503 (1883).

ward a rule above the legal categories which would classify the cases.

Brett thought recovery should be allowed because:

Whenever one person supplies goods or machinery, or the like for the purpose of their being used by another person under such circumstances that everyone of ordinary sense would, if he thought, recognize at once that unless he used ordinary care and skill with regard to the condition of the thing supplied or the mode of supplying it, there will be danger of injury to the person or property of him for whose use the thing is supplied, and who is to use it, a duty arises to use ordinary care and skill as to the condition or manner of supplying such thing.[31]

This statement was concocted by Brett from two types of cases: first, the case where two drivers or two ships are approaching each other and due care is required toward each other, and second, where a man is invited into a shop or warehouse and the owner must use reasonable care "to keep his house or warehouse that it may not endanger the person or property of the person invited." Since these two different situations resulted in the same legal rule, or stated differently, since two general principles when applied resulted in the same legal rule, Brett thought there must be "some larger proposition which involves and covers both set of circumstances." This was because "the logic of inductive reasoning requires that where two propositions lead to exactly similar premises there must be a more remote and larger premise which embraces both of the major propositions." Brett's rule of ordinary care ran into some difficulty in looking back at the *Langridge* case and its insistence on both fraud and direct dealing. But Brett said of the *Langridge* case, "It is not, it cannot be accurately reported," and in any event the fact that recovery was allowed on the basis of fraud "in no way negatives the

31 Ibid., at 510; see also rule as stated at 509.

proposition that the action might have been supported on the ground of negligence without fraud."

The majority opinion in *Heaven v. Pender*, while proceeding on the invitee point, and while refusing to follow Brett in his flight, agrees that liability for negligence follows when the instrument is dangerous "as a gun" or when the instrument is in such a condition as to cause danger "not necessarily incident to the use of such an instrument" and no due warning is given. Approving this statement, the New York court in 1908 held that the question of a manufacturer's negligence could be left to a jury where the plaintiff lost an eye due to the explosion of a bottle of aerated water.[32] The next year a defective coffee urn or boiler which blew up and killed a man was permitted to join the aerated bottle in the danger concept.[33] The coffee-urn case provided the occasion for explaining two of the names given the dangerous category. Given an "inherently dangerous" article, the court explained, a manufacturer becomes liable for negligent construction which, when added to its inherent characteristics, makes it "imminently dangerous."

The categories by now were fairly well occupied. The dangerous concept had in it a loaded gun, possibly a defective gun, mislabeled poison, defective hair wash, scaffolds, a defective coffee urn, and a defective aerated bottle. The not-dangerous category, once referred to as only latently dangerous, had in it a defective carriage, a bursting lamp, a defective balance wheel for a circular saw, and a defective boiler. Perhaps it is not too surprising to find a defective soldering lamp in *Blacker v. Lake*[34] joining the not-dangerous class. But the English court, in the opinions of its two judges, experienced some difficulty. For the first judge there appears to have been

[32] Torgesen v. Schultz, 192 N.Y. 156, 84 N.E. 956 (1908).

[33] Statler v. Ray, 195 N.Y. 478, 88 N.E. 1063 (1909).

[34] 106 L.T. 533 (1912).

no difficulty in classifying the soldering lamp as not dangerous. Yet the *Skivington* case caused trouble because it appeared to suggest that negligence could be substituted for
fraud and perhaps liability would follow even though the article was not dangerous. But in that event the *Skivington* case
should not be followed because it was in conflict with *Winterbottom v. Wright*. Accordingly, the soldering lamp not
being dangerous, it was error to leave the question of negligence to the jury. The second judge suggested a more surprising realignment of the cases which threatened the whole
danger category. He suggested that no recovery should be
permitted even though the lamp fell into the class of things
dangerous in themselves. The duty of the vendor in such a
case, he pointed out, would be a duty to warn, but that duty
is discharged if the nature of the article is obvious or known,
as was true in this case. Indeed, the *Skivington* and *Thomas v.
Winchester* cases were explainable on the very ground that
the articles appeared harmless and their contents were unknown. One might almost say that recovery was permitted in
those cases because the danger was only latent.

The period of the application of the doctrine of dangerous
articles as set forth in the *Longmeid* case and adopted in
Thomas v. Winchester may be thought to come to an end in
1915 with its application by a federal court—the Circuit Court
of Appeals for the Second Circuit. This was the way the law
looked to the court. "One who manufactures articles inherently dangerous, e.g. poisons, dynamite, gunpowder, torpe-
does, bottles of water under gas pressure, is liable in tort to
third parties which they injure, unless he has exercised reasonable care with reference to the articles manufactured. . . . On
the other hand, one who manufactures articles dangerous only
if defectively made, or installed, e.g., tables, chairs, pictures or
mirrors hung on the walls, carriages, automobiles, and so on is
not liable to third parties for injuries caused by them, except

in cases of willful injury or fraud."[35] Accordingly, the court denied recovery in a suit by the purchaser of a car from a dealer against the manufacturer when the front right wheel broke and the car turned over.

MacPherson v. Buick[36] begins the third phase of the life of the dangerous instrument concept. The New York Court of Appeals in 1916 had before it almost a repetition of the automobile case passed upon by the federal court the previous year. The plaintiff was driving his car, carrying a friend to the hospital, when the car suddenly collapsed due to a defective wheel. The plaintiff was seriously injured. The Buick Motor Company, the defendant, had sold the car to a retail dealer who in turn had sold it to the plaintiff. The defective wheel had been sold to the Buick company by the Imperial Wheel Company.

As was to be expected, counsel for the plaintiff urged that an automobile was "dangerous to a high degree."[37] It was, in fact, similar to a locomotive. It was much more like a locomotive than like a wagon. "The machine is a fair rival for the Empire Express," he said. "This is evidenced further by the fact that the person running an automobile must have a license of competency, equally with the locomotive engineer and by the legal restrictions imposed by law in the use of the automobile." It was "almost childish to say that an automobile at rest is not dangerous. Neither is a locomotive with the fire drawn" nor a battery of coffee boilers nor a 42-centimeter gun. The automobile, propelled by explosive gases, was "inherently dangerous." The trial judge had charged the jury that "an automobile is not an inherently dangerous vehicle"

[35] Cadillac v. Johnson, 221 Fed. 801, 803 (C.C.A. 2d, 1915).

[36] 217 N.Y. 382, 111 N.E. 1050 (1916); see Bohlen, Liability of Manufacturers to Persons Other than Their Immediate Vendors, 45 L.Q. Rev. 343 (1929).

[37] Brief for the Plaintiff 16, 17, 18.

but had said that they might find it "imminently dangerous if defective."[38] As to the difference between the two phrases, counsel said there was no point "juggling over definitions. 'Inherently' means 'inseparably.' 'Imminently' means 'threateningly.' " He did not comment on the request of the defendant that the judge charge the jury that recovery depended on the car being "eminently dangerous."[39] Counsel did write, however, that he "was powerfully impressed with a remark of Lord Chief Justice Isaacs, on his recent visit to this country, to the effect that in England they were getting away from merely abstract forms and were seeking to administer justice in each individual case."[40]

The New York Court of Appeals allowed recovery. Judge Cardozo recognized that "the foundations of this branch of the law . . . were laid in *Thomas v. Winchester.*" He said that some of the illustrations used in *Thomas v. Winchester* might be rejected today (having in mind no doubt the example of the defective carriage), but the principle of the case was the important thing. "There never has in this state been doubt or disavowal of the principle itself." Even while remarking that "precedents drawn from the days of travel by stagecoach do not fit the conditions of travel today," he was quick to add the explanation: "The principle that the danger must be imminent does not change, but the things subject to the principle do change." And in addition there were underlying principles. They were stated, more or less, Cardozo said, by Brett in *Heaven v. Pender.*

To be sure, Cardozo was not certain that this statement of underlying principles was an accurate exposition of the law of England. He thought "it may need some qualification even in our own state. Like most attempts at comprehensive defini-

---

[38] 217 N.Y. 382, 396, 111 N.E. 1050, 1055 (1916).

[39] Ibid., at 399, 1056.   [40] Brief for the Plaintiff 23.

tion, it may involve errors of inclusion and exclusion." He thought, however, that "its tests and standards, at least in their underlying principles, with whatever qualifications may be called for as they are applied to varying conditions, are the tests and standards of our law." He did not comment on the statement of Brett concerning *Thomas v. Winchester* that it "goes a very long way. I doubt whether it does not go too far."

As to the cases, Cardozo recognized that the early ones "suggest a narrow construction of the rule." He had reference to the boiler and balance-wheel cases. But the way to set them aside had already been shown. They could be distinguished because there the manufacturer had either pointed out the defect or had known that his test was not the final one. The distinction was based upon a point unsuccessfully advanced by losing counsel in *Winterbottom v. Wright*. Other cases showed that it was not necessary to be destructive in order to be dangerous. "A large coffee urn . . . may have within itself, if negligently made, the potency of danger, yet no one thinks of it as an implement whose normal function is destruction." And "what is true of the coffee urn is equally true of bottles of aerated water." *Devlin v. Smith* was important too. "A scaffold," Cardozo pointed out, "is not inherently a dangerous instrument." He admitted that the scaffold and the coffee-urn cases may "have extended the rule of *Thomas v. Winchester*," but "If so, this court is committed to the extension. The defendant argues that things inherently dangerous to life are poisons, explosives, deadly weapons, things whose normal function is to injure or destroy. But whatever the rule in *Thomas v. Winchester* may once have been, it has no longer that restricted meaning."

He showed a certain impatience for what he called "verbal niceties." He complained that "subtle distinctions are drawn by the defendant between things inherently dangerous and things imminently dangerous." As to this it was sufficient to say, "If danger was to be expected as reasonably certain, there was a duty of vigilance, and this whether you call the danger inherent or imminent." The rule was: "If the nature of a thing is such that it is reasonably certain to place life and limb in peril, when negligently made, it is then a thing of danger." But "there must be a knowledge of a danger not merely possible but probable." Thus what was only latently dangerous in *Thomas v. Winchester* now became imminently dangerous or inherently dangerous, or, if verbal niceties are to be disregarded, just plain or probably dangerous.

Elsewhere in commenting on the case, Cardozo seems to make somewhat less of the matter of principles. He wrote: "What, however, was the posture of affairs before the *Buick* case had been determined? Was there any law on the subject? A mass of judgments, more or less relevant, had been rendered by the same and other courts. A body of particulars existed in which an hypothesis might be reared. None the less, their implications were equivocal. . . . The things classified as dangerous have been steadily extended with a corresponding extension of the application of the remedy. . . . They have widened till they include a scaffold or an automobile or even pies and cakes when nails and other foreign substances have supplied ingredients not mentioned in the recipes of cook books." Cardozo described the legal process in connection with these cases as one in which "logic and utility still struggle for the mastery."[41] One can forgive Judge Cardozo for this language. It is traditional to think of logic as fighting with something. Sometimes it is thought of as fighting with history and experience.

In a reversal of itself, not so striking because the membership of the court was different, the same federal court hearing another appeal in the same case in which it had been decided

[41] Cardozo, The Growth of the Law 40–41, 76–78 (1924).

that a defective automobile was not inherently dangerous now stated with new wisdom: "We cannot believe that the liability of a manufacturer of an automobile has any analogy to the liability of a manufacturer of 'tables, chairs, pictures or mirrors hung on walls.' The analogy is rather that of a manufacturer of unwholesome food or of a poisonous drug."[42]

MacPherson v. Buick renamed and enlarged the danger category. It is usually thought to have brought the law into line with "social considerations."[43] But it did not remove the necessity for deciding cases. Later the New York courts were able to put into the category of things of danger or probably dangerous a defective bottle[44] and another coffee urn,[45] although one less terrifying than the coffee boiler of 1909. But for some reason or other, admission was denied to a defective automobile when the defect was a door handle which gave way, causing one of the doors to open with the result that the plaintiff was thrown through the door and under the car. The defective handle did not make the car a "thing of danger."[46] And if one is comparing cases and examples, it has to be admitted that a door handle is less closely connected with those things which make a car like a locomotive than is the wheel on which it runs.

Nevertheless, a new freedom follows from *MacPherson v. Buick*. Under it, as the Massachusetts court has said, the exception in favor of liability for negligence where the instrument is probably dangerous has swallowed up the purported rule that "a manufacturer or supplier is never liable for negli-

[42] Johnson v. Cadillac, 261 Fed. 878, 886 (C.C.A. 2d, 1919).

[43] See Torts: Liability of Manufacturer to Consumer for Article Dangerous Because of Defective Construction, 9 Corn. L. Q. 494 (1924).

[44] Smith v. Peerless Glass Co., 259 N.Y. 292, 181 N.E. 576 (1932); cf. Bates v. Batey & Co., [1913] 3 K.B. 351.

[45] Hoenig v. Central Stamping Co., 273 N.Y. 485, 6 N.E. 2d 415 (1936).

[46] Cohen v. Brockway Motor Corp., 240 App. Div. 18, 268 N.Y. Supp. 545 (1934).

gence to a remote vendee."[47] The exception now seems to have the same certainty the rule once had. The exception is now a general principle of liability which can be stated nicely in the Restatement, and text writers can criticize courts for not applying what is now an obvious rule of liability.[48]

A somewhat similar development has occurred in England. In *Donoghue v. Stevenson*[49] in 1932, the manufacturer of a bottle of ginger beer was held liable to the plaintiff who had purchased the bottle through a friend at a café. The bottle contained the decomposed remains of a snail. The opinions of the majority judges stressed the close and almost direct relationship between the manufacturer and the remote vendee. The control of the manufacturer of this type of article was thought to be "effective until the article reaches the consumer. . . . A manufacturer puts up an article of food in containers which he knows will be opened by the actual consumer. There can be no inspection by any purchaser and no reasonable preliminary inspection by the consumer." Lord Atkin, while stating that Brett's rule in *Heaven v. Pender* was too broad, found that the moral rule requiring the love of one's neighbour in law was translated into the injunction "you must not injure your neighbour." The question then was: "Who is my neighbour?" The practical rule evolved was of persons "closely and directly affected" and as to acts "which you can reasonably foresee would be likely to injure your neighbour." The emphasis on control and proximity revives the notion of the unconscious agent in *Langridge v. Levy*, as well as the inability to inspect, unsuccessfully urged in *Winterbottom v. Wright* and apparently implicit in the *Skivington* case.

As for other prior cases it was now said that the distinction

[47] Carter v. Yardley & Co., 319 Mass. 92, 64 N.E. 2d 693 (1946).

[48] See Harper, Law of Torts § 106 (1933).

[49] [1932] A.C. 562. Note the reference to trade names and patents at 583.

between things dangerous and those dangerous in themselves was "an unnatural one" and anyway the fact that there might be a special duty for one category no longer meant that a duty might not exist for others. *Winterbottom* and *Longmeid* were no longer controlling because negligence had not been alleged and proved in those cases. And as for the *Blacker* case, Lord Atkin had read and re-read it but had difficulty "in formulating the precise grounds upon which the judgment was given." Thus prior cases were realigned out of the way despite the protest of dissenting judges who adhered to the view of the exception only for dangerous articles in the more traditional sense.

While the emphasis was on continuing control in the *Donoghue* case, and counsel urged that the *Donoghue* case applied only to articles intended for internal consumption, its rule was applied in *Grant v. Australian Knitting Mills*[50] in 1936 to underpants defective due to the presence of an irritating chemical. Here the emphasis could be more on the point that the defect was hidden. While the *Blacker* case was in a sense disregarded, the point made by one of its judges was in fact accepted. Reasoning in a manner not unlike *Skivington*, which substituted negligence for fraud, the court put secrecy in the place of control. Donoghue's case was now seen not to "depend on the bottle being stopped and sealed; the essential point in this regard was that the article should reach the consumer or user subject to the same defect as it had when it left the manufacturer." The court realized that in applying its test of directness, control, proximity and hidden defect, "many difficult problems will arise. . . . Many qualifying conditions and many complications of fact may in the future come before the Courts for decision." But "in their Lordships' opinion it is enough for them to decide this case on its actual facts."

[50] [1936] A.C. 85.

With the breakdown of the inherently dangerous rule, the cycle from *Dixon v. Bell* was complete. But it would be a mistake to believe that the breakdown makes possible a general rule, such as the rule of negligence, which now can be applied. A rule so stated would be equivalent to the flight of Brett. Negligence itself must be given meaning by the examples to be included under it. Unlimited liability is not intended. As the comparison of cases proceeds, new categories will be stressed. Perhaps, for example, there will be a category for trade-marked, patented, advertised, or monopolized articles. The basis for such a category exists. The process of reasoning by example will decide.

III

It is customary to think of case-law reasoning as inductive and the application of statutes as deductive.[51] The thought seems erroneous but the emphasis has some meaning. With case law the concepts can be created out of particular instances. This is not truly inductive, but the direction appears to be from particular to general. It has been pointed out that the general finds its meaning in the relationship between the particulars. Yet it has the capacity to suggest by the implication of hypothetical cases which it carries and even by its ability to suggest other categories which sound the same. The phrase "imminent danger," for example, suggested immediacy, inherence, and eminence. To this extent, the phrase suggests the instances to be included under it, and something like deductive reasoning occurs. The new instances will still have to be weighed with the old, however, and the remaking of the concept word itself is apparent. It not only comes to have new meanings, but the word itself may change or disappear. The application of a statute seems to be in great contrast. The words are given. They are not to be taken lightly since they

[51] Allen, Law in the Making 249 (1930).

express the will of the legislature The legislature is the law-making body. It looks like deduction to apply the word to the specific case.

The difference is seen immediately when it is realized that the words of a statute are not dictum.[52] The legislature may have had a particular case uppermost in mind, but it has spoken in general terms. Not only respect but application is due to the general words the legislature used. The rules for statutory construction make the same point. They are words which tell one how to operate a given classification system. The problem is to place the species inside the genus and the particular case inside the species. The words used by the legislature are treated as words of classification which are to be applied. Yet the rules themselves show that there may be some ambiguity in the words used. The words are to be construed in the light of the meaning given to other words in the same or related statute. The specification of particular instances indicates that similar but unmentioned instances are not to be included. But the specification of particular instances, when in addition a word of a general category is used, may be the indication that other like instances are also intended; hence the *ejusdem generis* rule.

Thus in the application of a statute the intent of the legislature seems important. The rules of construction are ways of finding out the intent. The actual words used are important but insufficient. The report of congressional committees may give some clue. Prior drafts of the statute may show where meaning was intentionally changed. Bills presented but not passed may have some bearing. Words spoken in debate may now be looked at. Even the conduct of the litigants may be important in that the failure of the government to have acted over a period of time on what it now suggests as the proper

---

[52] But the statement of contradictory purposes may be; see Employment Act of 1946, 60 Stat. 24 (1946) as amended 60 Stat. 838 (1946), 15 U.S.C.A. §§ 1021-24 (Supp., 1947).

interpretation throws light on the common meaning. But it is not easy to find the intent of the legislature.[53]

Justice Reed has given us some Polonius-sounding advice on the matter:

There is, of course, no more persuasive evidence of the purpose of a statute than the words by which the legislature undertook to give expression to its wishes. Often these words are sufficient in and of themselves to determine the purpose of the legislature. In such cases we have followed their plain meaning. When that meaning had led to absurd or futile results, however, this Court has looked beyond the words to the purpose of the act. Frequently, however, even when the plain meaning did not produce absurd results but merely an unreasonable one "plainly at variance with the policy of legislation as a whole" this Court has followed that purpose rather than the literal words. When aid to construction of the meaning of words, as used in the statute, is available, there certainly can be no "rule of law" which forbids the use, however clear the words may appear on superficial examination. The interpretation of the meaning of statutes, as applied to justiciable controversies, is exclusively a judicial function. This duty requires one body of public servants, the judges, to construe the meaning of what another body, the legislators, has said. Obviously there is danger that the courts' conclusion as to legislative purpose will be unconsciously influenced by the judges' own views or by factors not considered by the enacting body. A lively appreciation of the danger is the best assurance of escape from its threat but hardly justifies an acceptance of a literal interpretation dogma which withholds from the courts available information for reaching a correct conclusion. Emphasis should be laid too upon the necessity for appraisal of the purposes as a whole of Congress in analyzing the meaning of clauses of sections of general acts. A few words of general connotation appearing in the text of statutes should not be given a wide meaning, contrary to settled policy, "except as a different purpose is plainly shown."[54]

The words of advice force one to re-examine whether there is any difference between case law and statutory interpretation. It is not enough to show that the words used by the leg-

[53] See Frankfurter, Some Reflections on the Reading of Statutes, 47 Col. L. Rev. 527 (1947).

[54] United States v. American Trucking Ass'n, 310 U.S. 534, 542 (1940).

islature have some meaning. Concepts created by case law also have some meaning, but the meaning is ambiguous. It is not clear how wide or narrow the scope is to be. Can it be said that the words used by the legislature have any more meaning than that, or is there the same ambiguity? One important difference can be noted immediately. Where case law is considered, there is a conscious realignment of cases; the problem is not the intention of the prior judge. But with a statute the reference is to the kind of things intended by the legislature. All concepts suggest, but case-law concepts can be re-worked. A statutory concept, however, is supposed to suggest what the legislature had in mind; the items to be included under it should be of the same order. We mean to accomplish what the legislature intended. This is what Justice Reed has said. The difficulty is that what the legislature intended is ambiguous. In a significant sense there is only a general intent which preserves as much ambiguity in the concept used as though it had been created by case law.

This is not the result of inadequate draftsmanship, as is so frequently urged. Matters are not decided until they have to be. For a legislature perhaps the pressures are such that a bill has to be passed dealing with a certain subject. But the precise effect of the bill is not something upon which the members have to reach agreement. If the legislature were a court, it would not decide the precise effect until a specific fact situation arose demanding an answer. Its first pronouncement would not be expected to fill in the gaps. But since it is not a court, this is even more true. It will not be required to make the determination in any event, but can wait for the court to do so.[55] There is a related and an additional reason for ambi-

---

[55] Cf. Frank, Words and Music: Some Reflections on Statutory Interpretation, 47 Col. L. Rev. 1259 (1947). Note that not every change in a court's statement of the statutory rule need be an actual change in the construction of the statute. Cf. United States v. Standard Oil Co. of New Jersey, 221 U.S. 1 (1911) and United States v. Addyston Pipe and Steel Co., 85 Fed. 271 (C.C.A. 6th, 1898).

guity. As to what type of situation is the legislature to make a decision? Despite much gospel to the contrary, a legislature is not a fact-finding body. There is no mechanism, as there is with a court, to require the legislature to sift facts and to make a decision about specific situations. There need be no agreement about what the situation is. The members of the legislative body will be talking about different things; they cannot force each other to accept even a hypothetical set of facts. The result is that even in a non-controversial atmosphere just exactly what has been decided will not be clear.

Controversy does not help. Agreement is then possible only through escape to a higher level of discourse with greater ambiguity. This is one element which makes compromise possible. Moreover, from the standpoint of the individual member of the legislature there is reason to be deceptive. He must escape from pressures at home. Newspapers may have created an atmosphere in which some legislation must be passed. Perhaps the only chance to get legislation through is to have it mean something not understood by some colleagues. If the court in construing the legislation is going to look at committee reports and remarks during debates, words which would be voted down if included in the bill will be used on the floor or in a report as a kind of illicit and, it is hoped, effective legislation. And if all this were not sufficient, it cannot be forgotten that to speak of legislative intent is to talk of group action, where much of the group may be ignorant or misinformed. Yet the emphasis should not be on this fact, but on the necessity that there be ambiguity before there can be any agreement about how unknown cases will be handled.

But the court will search for the legislative intent, and this does make a difference. Its search results in an initial filling-up of the gap. The first opinions may not definitely set the whole interpretation. A more decisive view may be edged toward, but finally there is likely to be an interpretation by the court which gives greater content to the words used. In building up this interpretation, the reference will be to the kind of examples that the words used, as commonly understood, would call to mind. Reasoning by example will then proceed from that point. There is a difference then from case law in that the legislature has compelled the use of one word. The word will not change verbally. It could change in meaning, however, and if frequent appeals as to what the legislature really intended are permitted, it may shift radically from time to time. When this is done, a court in interpreting legislation has really more discretion than it has with case law. For it can escape from prior cases by saying that they have ignored the legislative intent.

There is great danger in this. Legislatures and courts are co-operative law-making bodies. It is important to know where the responsibility lies. If legislation which is disfavored can be interpreted away from time to time, then it is not to be expected, particularly if controversy is high, that the legislature will ever act. It will always be possible to say that new legislation is not needed because the court in the future will make a more appropriate interpretation. If the court is to have freedom to reinterpret legislation, the result will be to relieve the legislature from pressure. The legislation needs judicial consistency. Moreover, the court's own behavior in the face of pressure is likely to be indecisive. In all likelihood it will do enough to prevent legislative revision and not much more. Therefore it seems better to say that once a decisive interpretation of legislative intent has been made, and in that sense a direction has been fixed within the gap of ambiguity, the court should take that direction as given. In this sense a court's interpretation of legislation is not dictum. The words it uses do more than decide the case. They give broad direction to the statute.

The doctrine which is suggested here is a hard one. In many

controversial situations, legislative revision cannot be expected. It often appears that the only hope lies with the courts. Yet the democratic process seems to require that controversial changes should be made by the legislative body. This is not only because there is a mechanism for holding legislators responsible. It is also because courts are normally timid. Since they decide only the case before them, it is difficult for them to compel any controversial reform unless they are willing to hold to an unpopular doctrine over a sustained period of time. The difficulties which administrative agencies have in the face of sustained pressure serve as a warning. When courts enter the area of great controversy, they require unusual protection. They must be ready to appeal to the constitution.

Where legislative interpretation is concerned, therefore, it appears that legal reasoning does attempt to fix the meaning of the word. When this is done, subsequent cases must be decided upon the basis that the prior meaning remains. It must not be re-worked. Its meaning is made clear as examples are seen, but the reference is fixed. It is a hard doctrine against which judges frequently rebel. The Mann Act is a good example.[56]

On June 25, 1910, the Mann Act, which recites that it "shall be known and referred to as the 'White Slave Traffic Act,'" went into effect. The Act[57] provides in part: "Any person who shall knowingly transport or cause to be transported, or aid or assist in obtaining transportation for, or in transporting, in interstate or foreign commerce or in any territory or in the District of Columbia, any woman or girl for the purpose of prostitution or debauchery, or for any other

[56] See also for the problem of legislative intent, Radin, A Case Study in Statutory Interpretation: Western Union Co. v. Lenroot, 33 Calif. L. Rev. 219 (1945).

[57] 36 Stat. 825 (1910), 18 U.S.C.A. § 398 (1927).

immoral purpose, or with the intent and purpose to induce, entice or compel such woman or girl to become a prostitute, or to give herself up to debauchery, or to engage in any other immoral practice . . . shall be deemed guilty of a felony." The Act was not passed in haste. Indeed, the matter was much debated and prior reports about it had been written. The Secretary of Commerce and Labor had discussed the problem in his 1908 report; so had an Immigration Commission in a preliminary report for 1909. There were international aspects to the problem, and a treaty had been concluded. The President had directed the attention of Congress to the need for legislation, and the proposed bill had been considered in majority and minority congressional committee reports.

The Mann Act was passed during a period when large American cities had illegal but segregated "red-light" areas. It was believed that women were procured for houses of prostitution by bands of "white slavers" who "were said to operate from coast to coast, in town and country, with tentacles in foreign lands, east and west and across the American borders. The most sensational of these were said to be the French, Italian, and Jewish rings who preyed on innocent girls of their respective nationalities at ports of entry into the United States or ensnared them at the ports of embarkation in Europe and even in their home towns." It was thought that the girls were young; many of them were supposed to be "scarcely in their teens."[58] They were forced or lured into the business. It was thought that they had previously been virtuous, and while supposedly many of them had been aliens, it was also believed that they represented "our" women. Once captured, the woman disappeared from her own community, was brutally treated, whipped with rawhide, and became, as the House Report said, practically a slave in the true sense of the word.[59]

[58] Reckless, Vice in Chicago 40 (1933).
[59] H.R. Rep. 47, 61st Cong. 2d Sess. (1909).

To meet this assumed situation, the White Slave Traffic Act made it a crime to transport a woman "for the purpose of prostitution, or debauchery or for any other immoral purpose."

While Representative Richardson said that the bill was "impractical, vague, indistinct and indefinite in every respect,"[60] the debates show that Congress had in mind some very fundamental issues. On one side were those who were in favor of home rule or the powers of the states. Congressman Bartlett of Illinois was on this side. He said that he found himself compelled to resist the enactment of a measure "like this, behind which are gathered . . . so many forces of morality, piety and reform."[61] But in his voting he was guided by "the great white light steadily stream[ing] out of the Constitution,"[62] and he thought that the "States still have the police powers to prevent in their borders the offenses against morality so eloquently denounced by the advocates of this bill. . . . If any man lives in a State which fails in its duty to enact such laws, I submit that under our system of government his first duty is at home."[63] On the other side were those who argued that "public health and public morals appeal to us." They were the ones who said, "The proposed legislation is constitutional, and it is related to moral considerations of the most compelling force. If it were not true that our penal legislation were related to moral questions, and moral considerations, then the whole fabric of that legislation would lose its power to command the approbation of the country."[64] They were careful to insist, however, that "the sections proposed do not amount to an interference with the police powers of the States."[65]

[60] 45 Cong. Rec. 810 (1910).
[61] 45 Cong. Rec. App. 11 (1910).   [63] Ibid.
[62] Ibid.   [64] 45 Cong. Rec. 1040 (1910).
[65] H.R. Rep. 47, 61st Cong. 2d Sess., at 4 (1909).

In a way the bill must surely have been about the "white-slave traffic." Congressman Mann at the end of the debate emphasized the subject matter by declaring: "Congress would be derelict in its duty if it did not exercise [power], because all the horrors which have been urged, either truthfully or fancifully, against the black-slave traffic pale into insignificance as compared with the horrors of the so-called 'white-slave traffic.' "[66] Congressman Peters said: "The considerations which prompt the support of this bill are so widespread and its objects are so well understood and meet with such universal approval that no explanation or repetition of them need be made to this House. The bill aims to aid in the suppression of the white-slave traffic. . . ."[67] The majority report of the House Committee had defined the white-slave trade as the "business of securing white women and girls and selling them outright or exploiting them for immoral purposes."[68] It had stressed the international character of the trade and the large earnings involved.

Yet while it was said that "the traffic at which this bill strikes is admitted to be abhorrent to all men," and "the time will never arrive when there will be a change of sentiment with respect to its infamy and depravity,"[69] there was confusion both as to the facts and as to the legislation proposed.

For example, Congressman Richardson said he knew of the complaint about the traffic but "it may be that there is a good deal of exaggeration about it." Many of the situations described in the House Report had to do with conditions in Illinois. But the "law in Illinois has been strengthened and there had been many prosecutions under it."[70] Congressman Adamson noted that "the Chairman of the Committee on Immigration and Naturalization . . . stated . . . that the white

[66] 45 Cong. Rec. 1040 (1910).   [67] Ibid., at 1035.
[68] H.R. Rep. 47, 61st Cong. 2d Sess., at 11 (1909).
[69] 45 Cong. Rec. 1039 (1910).   [70] Ibid., at 810.

slave traffic had practically been stamped out of our large cities." An examination of the instances cited, Adamson thought, would show that they could be handled under existing laws.[71] And despite the descriptions of immorality, the truth was that society was getting better and "we are vastly better morally than the rest of the world." On the other hand, Congressman Russell, as his contribution on the facts, told the House the story of a Negro who was supposed to have purchased his third white wife "out of a group of twenty-five that were offered for sale in Chicago."[72]

Whatever the evil, presumably the legislation was molded to cure it. The Act speaks of "prostitution," "debauchery," and of "other immoral practice" or "purpose." So far as prostitution was concerned, the report of the House Committee had said that "the bill reported does not endeavor to regulate, prohibit or punish prostitution or the keeping of places where prostitution is indulged in." Congressman Adamson noted that the purpose of the bill "is not to stamp out prostitution, nor do its advocates so contend." He realized that many good men and women, and some good congressmen, thought the purpose was to stamp out prostitution and immorality, but this was an error. But the House Report clearly said that the bill reaches the transportation of women "for the purpose of prostitution." And Representative Peters joined the three elements of white-slave traffic, transportation, and prostitution together in his statement that "the bill aims to aid in the suppression of the white slave traffic by making it a felony to purchase interstate transportation for any woman going to a place for purposes of prostitution."[73]

So far as debauchery was concerned, perhaps it was a mistake to believe that the bill looked to the protection of female virtue. Congressman Adamson said that if it had "we would unanimously support it. But no such pretense even is made.

---

[71] Ibid., at 1031.   [72] Ibid., at 821.   [73] Ibid., at 1035.

The only professed and possible purpose of this legislation is to purify interstate commerce."

It was perhaps strange then that "there is no attempt to prohibit a vile man from buying a ticket to be used by himself or another vile man for transportation into another State for the purpose of immorality."[74] Nevertheless, carried to its last analysis, the proposition underlying the bill "would endeavor to exclude all vile and impure people from the use of interstate facilities for commerce. . . . There would be a wide field of different opinion as to who was vile and impure and what practices constituted immorality." Somewhat along the same line, the minority report in the Senate urged, "It would be intolerable that the person from whom they purchased a railroad ticket should inquire as to the morality or chastity" of the person who was to use the ticket.[75]

Except for the charge that the provisions of the bill were "liable to furnish boundless opportunity to hold up and blackmail and make unnecessary trouble without the corresponding benefit to society,"[76] there seemed to be general agreement that the women involved were victims. The women were under control of keepers and were unable to communicate with the outside world without permission.[77] It was said that the evidence "shows, that many victims of this traffic, have been coerced into leading lives of shame, by the use of force, deceit, fraud and every variety of trickery. In many instances they are most unwilling victims, who are literally compelled to practice immorality, and are held to its pursuit by means of violence and restraint."[78] The House Report said that in many cases the women "are practically slaves in the true sense of the word." Something of the flavor of the debate is indicated by Congressman Adamson's denunciation of the idea

[74] Ibid., at 1033.
[75] Ibid., at 941.
[76] Ibid., at 1033.
[77] Ibid., at 811.
[78] Ibid., at 1037.

that "woman's condition of vileness . . . is contagious of contact" and "the horrible falsehood that women are creatures per se vile and immoral designed and intended in nature for no other than immoral purposes." This was to show that women were not like diseased animals or persons or like lottery tickets which, as a constitutional matter, could be kept out of interstate commerce. Rather women were the "sweet and lovely partners of our joys and sorrows."[79] The reporter notes applause.

There was hardly any discussion of the meaning of "other immoral practice" or "purpose." It was known to some that in 1908, in the *Bitty* case, the Supreme Court had construed similar language in a related statute which dealt with alien women imported for the purpose of prostitution or "any other immoral purpose" to include the importation of a woman for the purpose of concubinage. At least it was known to Congressman Richardson, who, however, thought the Mann Act unconstitutional. He said the Court in the *Bitty* case had given the phrase "a broad, liberal and wise construction in order to uphold morality."[80] The House Report mentions the *Bitty* case but states that it does so "only in passing."[81]

The law was to apply in the District of Columbia "without regard to the crossing of district, territorial or state lines."[82] But at least not every congressman recognized what the application would be. Some who opposed the bill said they would be in favor of legislation "abolishing bawdy houses in the District of Columbia."[83] One who was in favor of the bill but had been twitted for not advocating such a remedy before for the District defended himself by saying that he was not

[79] Ibid., at 1033.   [80] Ibid., at 809.

[81] H.R. Rep. 47, 61st Cong. 2d Sess., at 7 (1909).

[82] S. Rep. 866, 61st Cong. 2d Sess., at 2 (1910). The report is almost identical with the House Report.

[83] 45 Cong. Rec. App. 12 (1910).

"a self-constituted, pestiferous reformer."[84] And Congressman Borland, who introduced an anti-pandering bill for the District at about the same time, stated flatly, over the objections of Representative Mann, that the Mann Act did not cover the subject in the District but "was designed to regulate the national part of it . . . and could regulate nothing else."[85]

The Mann Act was passed after there had been many extensive governmental investigations. Yet there was no common understanding of the facts, and whatever understanding seems to have been achieved concerning the white-slave trade in retrospect seems incorrectly based. The words used were broad and ambiguous. There were three key phrases; "prostitution," "debauchery," and "for any other immoral purpose." The Act was now ready for interpretation.

By 1913, prostitution and debauchery had been applied by the Supreme Court.

Hoke and Economides[86] had been indicted for inducing a woman "to go in interstate commerce . . . for the purpose of prostitution." They raised the question of the constitutionality of the Act. Reasoning by analogy, Justice McKenna said, ". . . surely if the facility of interstate transportation can be taken away from the demoralization of lotteries, the debasement of obscene literature, the contagion of diseased cattle or persons, the impurity of food and drugs, the like facility can be taken away from the systematic enticement to and the enslavement in prostitution and debauchery of women, and, more insistently of girls." The construction, of course, emphasized the involuntary nature of the woman's conduct, the system involved, presumably organized traffic, and the belief that many of the women were minors.

On the same day as the opinion in *Hoke and Economides,*

---

[84] Ibid., at 1040.   [85] Ibid., at 3138.
[86] Hoke and Economides v. United States, 227 U.S. 308 (1913).

Justice McKenna in *Athanasaw v. United States*[87] upheld the application of the Act through the word "debauchery" to a defendant who had caused a girl to be transported from Georgia to Florida for the ostensible purpose of appearing as a chorus girl in a theater operated by the defendant. There was evidence of improper advances made to the girl upon her arrival; the advances were related to her membership in the theater group. The Supreme Court held that debauchery as used in the Act did not mean only sexual intercourse but "was designed to reach acts which might ultimately lead to that phase of debauchery which consisted in 'sexual actions.' " But the Circuit Court of Appeals said that this case and *Hoke and Economides* taken together "were so strong as to amount to a direct decision on the point" that the White Slave Traffic Act was not confined to cases of white slavery.[88]

Then in 1915 the Supreme Court apparently held that the Act was not confined to cases where the woman was "practically a slave."[89] The Court had before it an indictment of a woman for conspiracy. The conspiracy charged was between the woman and one Laudenschlager that Laudenschlager should "cause the defendant [the woman] to be transported from Illinois to Wisconsin for the purpose of prostitution." It was urged that since the woman could not commit the substantive crime of violating the Mann Act, for she would be the victim transported, she could not be guilty of conspiracy to commit that crime. But Justice Holmes held that she could be. He did not agree that the woman victim would never be under the prohibition of the Mann Act. He said, "Suppose, for instance that a professional prostitute, as well able to look out for herself as was the man, should suggest and

[87] 227 U.S. 326 (1913).

[88] Hays v. United States, 231 Fed. 106 (C.C.A. 8th, 1916); the case later became one of the Caminetti cases.

[89] United States v. Holte, 236 U.S. 140 (1915).

carry out the journey within the act of 1910 in the hope of blackmailing the man, and should buy the railroad tickets, or should pay the fare from Jersey City to New York, she would be within the letter of the act of 1910 and we see no reason why the act should not be held to apply." Therefore "we see equally little reason for not treating the preliminary agreement as a conspiracy that the law can reach, if we abandon the illusion that the woman always is the victim. The words of the statute punish the transportation of a woman for the purpose of prostitution even if she were the first to suggest the crime."

The Court took the view that the woman could be punished over the objections of Justices Lamar and Day, who dissented in part on constitutional grounds: "Congress had no power to punish immorality." If then the "woman could be so punished for conspiring with her slaver, the fundamental idea that makes the act valid would be destroyed. She would cease to be an object of traffic . . . so as to be subject to regulative prohibitions under the Commerce Clause—but would be voluntarily travelling on her own account. . . ."

It became clear in the *Caminetti* cases[90] in 1917, when the Supreme Court applied the phrase "for any other immoral purpose," that organized traffic did not have to be involved either. The indictments considered in *Caminetti* involved the transportation of women for the purpose of paid cohabitation or for the purpose of having them become mistress and concubine. But the indictments did not involve commercialized and organized vice.

Counsel for the defendants urged against this conclusion the legislative history of the law as well as its given title. They referred to the House Committee Report to "demonstrate that commercial traffic alone was in view."[91] They pointed to what

[90] Caminetti v. United States, 242 U.S. 470 (1917).
[91] Ibid., at 474.

they termed "an unofficial communication to one of his subordinates" by the Attorney General in which they claimed that the Attorney General said that the legislation "does not attempt to regulate the practice of voluntary prostitution but aims solely to prevent panderers and procurers" from plying their infamous trade. This was "the full equivalent of saying that the law does not apply to those who indulge their own passions merely for their own gratification, but applies solely to those who engage in the trade of pandering to the passions of others."[92] Not only was the vice not organized and commercialized, but the women were not inexperienced victims. In one case, while there was conflicting testimony before the jury, there was some evidence that the woman was doing the pursuing. Another case was described by counsel as follows:

... the woman was a public prostitute and made no pretense of virtue. Hays happened to meet her at Oklahoma City while attending a cattlemen's convention there, and after his return to his home another woman telegraphed the Oklahoma woman to come to Kansas, sending her the money with which to buy the ticket. In response to that message the woman went from Oklahoma City to Wichita, where she met and entertained Hays. We may justly censure the man for associating with those loose women, but that was the extent of his offense, for there is not, so far as the woman in this case is concerned, a single aggravating circumstance; and yet this man of good standing in the community where he lives, with a wife and children dependent on him, has been sentenced to the penitentiary for eighteen months, stripped of his civil rights, his wife deprived of his support, his boy and girl forever branded as the children of a convict, and all for no better reason than that he made a mistake which the State of Kansas might have adequately punished by a fine. To subject American citizens to such punishments for such offenses will brutalize the American people in time, and to suppose that the American Congress intended such a result impeaches its wisdom as well as its sense of justice.[93]

[92] Petition for Rehearing 14, 15.

[93] Ibid., at 18, 19.

The result would be:

> ...that for every man who can be convicted under this statute, when charged with only an immorality, two men will submit to extortion and pay blood-money to save themselves, their families, and their friends from the humiliation which an exposure of their mistakes would bring.[94]

The prosecution placed its case on the plain meaning of the phrase "prostitution, or debauchery, or other immoral purpose." It agreed that "other immoral purpose" included "words of such generality that a criminal conviction thereunder could not be tolerated for acts whose purpose was any and every sort of immorality." The words "must be limited to that genus of which the preceding descriptions are species." The problem was to find the genus. And the defendants' contention that the genus was "commercialized vice" was wrong because, while prostitution involved the financial element, debauchery did not, since it only involved "a leading of a chaste girl into unchastity. . . . The nexus indicative of the genus is sexual immorality."[95] The conclusion was fortified by the *Bitty* case. Moreover, if the genus were restricted to commercialized vice, the class would be exhausted by prostitution and debauchery and the words "immoral purpose" and "immoral practice" would "be rendered impotent. If the particular words exhaust the genus there is nothing *ejusdem generis* left, and in such case we must give the general words a meaning outside of the class. . . ."[96]

It would be wrong, the prosecution contended, to resort to the title or the legislative history.[97] "It would transcend judicial power to insert limitations or conditions upon dis-

---

[94] Ibid., at 20.

[95] Caminetti v. United States, Brief for United States 15.

[96] Ibid., at 16, quoting United States v. Mescall, 215 U.S. 26, 31, 32 (1909).

[97] Ibid., at 11, 12, quoting MacKenzie v. Hare, 239 U.S. 299, 308 (1908).

putable considerations of reasons which impelled the law, or of conditions to which it might be conjectured it was addressed and intended to accommodate." Moreover, so far as the debates were concerned, "the writer of a bill may explain his purpose to his fellow members, and they may vote for it solely because in their judgment it has a wider or narrower scope than he states."

According to Justice Day, there was "no ambiguity in the terms of this Act." The words "immoral purpose" had been interpreted by the Court in a related and earlier act and that interpretation "must be presumed to have been known to Congress when it enacted the law here involved." Under the *Bitty* case[98] "immoral purpose" included importing a woman for the purpose of concubinage. The Act there read "that the importation into the United States of any alien woman or girl for the purpose of prostitution, or for any other immoral purpose, is hereby forbidden." And the Court had then said that "the immoral purpose charged in the indictment is of the same general class or kind as the one that controls in the importation of an alien woman for the purpose strictly of prostitution. The prostitute may, in the popular sense, be more degraded in character than the concubine, but the latter none the less must be held to lead an immoral life, if any regard whatever be had to the views that are almost universally held in this country as to the relations which may rightfully, from the standpoint of morality, exist between man and woman in the matter of sexual intercourse."

The Court said it was giving effect to the "common understanding" and "plain import" of the words which could not be changed by reference to the House Committee report or the title. Moreover, the fact that the "Act as it is written opens the door to blackmailing operations upon a large scale, is no

[98] United States v. Bitty, 208 U.S. 393 (1908).

reason why the courts should refuse to enforce it according to its terms."[99]

At the very least, *Caminetti* set the direction of the Mann Act to include more than white slavery; at most it imported into the statute all acts commonly thought to be sexually immoral. The suggested definition of "any other immoral purpose" went far beyond the facts to include those things which "common understanding" or views "almost universally held in this country" would regard as immoral in the matter of sexual intercourse. This wide interpretation seems to have been accepted by Chief Justice Taft in a case involving the Motor Vehicle Theft Act.[100] He referred to the Mann Act as dealing with "prostitution or concubinage and other forms of immorality." The image of women under control of keepers had apparently disappeared. Justice Stone in 1932, while holding that mere acquiescence by a woman would not subject her to a conspiracy conviction, said flatly, "Congress set out in the Mann Act to deal with cases which frequently, if not normally, involve consent and agreement on the part of the woman to the forbidden transportation."[101] Yet the actual

[99] Justice McKenna wrote a dissenting opinion concurred in by Chief Justice White and Justice Clark. "Language, even when most masterfully used, may miss sufficiency and give room for dispute. Is it a wonder therefore, that when used in the haste of legislation, in view of conditions perhaps only partly seen or not seen at all, the consequences, it may be, beyond present foresight, it often becomes necessary to apply the rule [of legislative intent although contrary to the literal language]?" The report of the committee had a "higher quality than debates on the floor of the House. . . . Blackmailers, of both sexes have arisen, using the terrors of the construction now sanctioned by this court as a help—indeed the means for their brigandage. The result is grave and should give us pause." 242 U.S. 470, 501, 502 (1918). As for the Bitty case, the statute there was different. For it was an amendment to a prior statute which prohibited the importation of any alien woman or girl into the United States for the "purposes of prostitution." When the amendment "or any other immoral purpose" was added, it was necessarily an enlargement upon the former.

[100] Brooks v. United States, 267 U.S. 432 (1925).

[101] Gebardi v. United States, 287 U.S. 112, 121 (1932); the Gebardi case was strikingly a local police matter.

facts of the *Caminetti* cases did involve paid prostitution or concubinage, and also, it would be easy to argue, some form of coercion, although not the coercion of white slavery. There was a wide difference between the facts and the broad doctrine of all sexual immorality. A good deal of ambiguity remained.

Surely no member of the Mann Act Congress had thought about such facts as were involved in the *Mortensen* case.[102] It was true that the petitioners operated a house of prostitution in Grand Island, Nebraska. They were husband and wife. But "in 1940 they planned an automobile trip to Salt Lake City, Utah, in order to visit Mrs. Mortensen's parents. Two girls who were employed by petitioners as prostitutes asked to be taken along for a vacation and the Mortensens agreed to their request. They motored to Yellowstone National Park and then on to Salt Lake City, where they all stayed at a tourist camp for four or five days. They visited Mrs. Mortensen's parents, and, in addition, the girls 'went to shows and around in the parks' and saw various other parts of the city. The four then returned in petitioners' automobile to Grand Island; on arrival they drove immediately to petitioners' house of ill fame and retired to their respective rooms." It was easy to argue that at the halfway point of the trip, namely when the journey back from Salt Lake City began, the girls were being transported to Grand Island for an immoral purpose. It was also easy to urge on the other side that "the sole purpose of the journey from beginning to end was to provide innocent recreation," and in any event the interstate commerce journey was hardly "a calculated means for effectuating sexual immorality" since, from all that appeared, leaving the girls in Grand Island would have worked just as well. The Supreme Court had difficulty with the case but in a five-to-four decision refused to uphold the conviction.

[102] Mortensen v. United States, 322 U.S. 369 (1944).

The majority opinion went on the ground that the purpose of the trip was innocent. "In ordinary speech an interstate trip undertaken for an innocent vacation purpose constitutes the use of interstate commerce for that innocent purpose." And surely if one thinks of the vacation category one need not think of the immoral purpose concept. But more seems to be implied in the vacation concept than the surface innocent purpose doctrine. There was nothing, Justice Murphy said, to show that "petitioners forced the girls against their will to return to Grand Island for immoral purposes." He said:

> We do not here question or reconsider any previous construction placed on the Act which may have led the federal government into areas of regulation not originally contemplated by Congress. But experience with the administration of the law admonishes us against adding another chapter of statutory construction and application which would have a similar effect and which would make possible even further justification of the fear expressed at the time of the adoption of the legislation that its broad provisions "are liable to furnish boundless opportunity to hold up and blackmail and make unnecessary trouble without any corresponding benefits to society."

> To punish those who transport inmates of a house of prostitution on an innocent vacation trip in no way related to the practice of their commercial vice is consistent neither with the purpose nor with the language of the Act. Congress was attempting primarily to eliminate the "white slave" business which uses interstate and foreign commerce as a means of procuring and distributing its victims and "to prevent panderers and procurers from compelling thousands of women and girls against their will and desire to enter and continue in a life of prostitution." Such clearly was not the situation revealed by the facts of this case.[103]

The *Mortensen* case, in other words, reveals a revolt against *Caminetti*. The fear of blackmail, the knowledge that Congress intended to eliminate white slavery, and the lack of

[103] Ibid., at 376.

compulsion for the pleasure trip made the vacation and the trip back innocent. Yet *Mortensen* was more closely connected with the business of commercialized vice, since, after all, petitioners were running a house of prostitution, than were the *Caminetti* cases.

But if the cross-country pleasure trip of the Mortensens was outside the Act, what of a four-block trip within the District of Columbia, paid for by the employer of a prostitute? The problem arose in the *Beach* case.[104] The defendant operated a dress shop. She employed a girl as her assistant; the girl lived with her, and on the suggestion of the defendant that the girl could earn more money by "selling herself," the girl agreed to work for the defendant as a prostitute. The fatal trip was a trip in a taxicab paid for by the defendant, who accompanied the girl to the Hotel Hamilton four blocks away from the apartment for the purpose of prostitution. The Circuit Court of Appeals for the District reversed the conviction.[105] Stating that local laws for the District covered the matter so completely that "about the only place in which the act can be done without running athwart the local law is in an anchored balloon," Chief Justice Groner found that the congressional purpose both at the time of the passage of the Mann Act and since, as indicated by subsequent local laws, was that the White Slavery Traffic Act was not to apply within the District except for conduct having an interstate aspect. The literal language was against him, Chief Justice Groner admitted. But there was some legislative history as to the Mann Act itself to support him; there were subsequent enactments; there was Justice Murphy's "well-considered Supreme Court dictum" in the *Mortensen* case, and "furthermore, once we apply locally the provisions of the Mann Act, we should

[104] United States v. Beach, 324 U.S. 193 (1945).

[105] 144 F. 2d 533 (App. D.C., 1944).

also be required to accept the results implicit in the doctrine
of the *Caminetti* case."[106]

The Supreme Court thought otherwise. In a majority *per
curiam* opinion, it held that "Congress, in enacting the Mann
Act, made it perfectly clear by its Committee Reports . . .
that it was intended to apply to transportation taking place
wholly within the District. . . ." In answer to the dissenting
opinion which followed, it said, "No other question was considered or decided below or discussed in the briefs and arguments of counsel here, and we decide no other." While it is
not clear that the argument was so strictly limited, the main
thrust of the defendant's position was that purely local matters
were not to be covered. In addition to pointing to the legislative history, the defendant said there had been "a uniform,
established custom for more than a quarter of a century . . .
never to prosecute under the Mann White Slave Act for a
transportation wholly within the boundaries of the District of
Columbia."[107]

---

[106] Chief Justice Groner quoted the following language from the dissent
of Justice Frankfurter in United States v. Monia, 317 U.S. 424, 432 (1943):
"A statute like any other living organism, derives significance and sustenance
from its environment, from which it cannot be severed without being muti-
lated. Especially is this true where the statute like the one before us, is part
of a legislative process having a history and a purpose. The meaning of such
a statute cannot be gained by confining inquiry within its four corners."

[107] United States v. Beach, Brief in Opposition to Certiorari 15–17. "At the
outset of the enforcement of the Mann White Slave Act the Department
of Justice took an official attitude that only cases involving commercialism
should be prosecuted. Despite the Diggs-Caminetti cases decided by this
Court on January 15, 1917, the Department of Justice in Circular No. 647,
issued January 26, 1917, drew attention to the fact that the Department policy would not be altered and instructed the United States Attorneys as
follows: 'This decision does not seem to admit of any change in the general
policy that has been prosecuted in the past six years with satisfactory results
in the enforcement of this law. On July 28, 1911 (Department File 145825-
65) Attorney General Wickersham said: "Such a case (concubinage) would
fall technically within the statute . . . in the application of the law federal
courts must be careful . . . to prevent them being turned into ordinary
courts of quarterly sessions to deal with . . . *violations of the police regula-*

The dissent of Justice Murphy was much more central. Surely the Act applied to white-slave traffic solely within the District. The difficulty was that there was no white slavery, and the prostitution was voluntary. The prior construction of the Act had been erroneous, ignoring the "plain Congressional purpose" with the result of punishing "anyone transporting a woman for immoral purposes quite apart from any connec-

---

tions of the community which should be dealt with by the local tribunals." [Italics supplied.] From the beginning District Attorneys have been advised by the Department as follows: "As to specific cases the Department must rely upon the discretion of the District Attorneys who have firsthand knowledge of the facts and an opportunity for personal interviews with the witnesses . . . and what reasons, if any, exist for thinking the ends of justice will be better served by the prosecution under federal law than under the laws of the state having jurisdiction." As a guide to the exercise of his discretion in non-commercial cases, you are advised that cases involving a fraudulent over-reaching or involving previously chaste or very young women or girls (when state laws are inadequate) involving married women (with young children) then living with their husbands, may properly receive consideration; that blackmail cases should, so far as possible, be avoided and that whenever the woman herself, voluntarily and without any over-reaching, has consented to the criminal arrangements, she, too, if the case shall seem to demand it, may be prosecuted as a conspirator.' That administrative policy of the Department of Justice has been continued to date. There has been a uniform, established custom for more than a quarter century indulged in on the part of the United State Government never to prosecute under the Mann White Slave Act for a transportation wholly within the boundaries of the District of Columbia. Not only has there been a non-use of the Federal Power to prosecute locally in the District of Columbia under the Mann White Slave Act but public policy has also favored such inaction. In the District of Columbia the offense of fornication has a maximum statutory penalty of $100 or six months, or both, and the offense of adultery is likewise a misdemeanor. It would seem absurd, therefore, with the light punishments for those crimes to contend that Congress intended that a taxicab ride of 3½ blocks, with the incidental feature of transportation wholly within the District of Columbia, would transform those misdemeanors into a heinous and loathsome felony having an extreme punishment."
But note the Government's petition for certiorari stated at pages 4, 5: "As the United States Attorney showed in a supplemental memorandum in support of a motion for rehearing in the court below, it has previously been assumed that the Act applies to transportation within the District of Columbia. Although, as he pointed out, it is impossible to ascertain the exact number of prosecutions based upon that theory, he referred specifically to four such provisions in the years 1936-1937."

tion with white-slavery." The result would be blackmail and unjust punishment. "No principle of stare decisis and no rule of statute or reason can justify such a result." The Court had added "another instance of tortured and grotesque application" to the "already unhappy history" of the statute.

It was possible to dispose of the *Beach* case because of the limited point deemed raised and stressed without rethinking either *Caminetti* or its broad doctrine that the statute included all acts commonly thought to be sexually immoral. *Cleveland v. United States*[108] permitted no such dodge. The defendants were Mormons who believed in and practiced polygamy. They had transported plural wives across state lines; prosecution under the Mann Act followed. The convictions were affirmed.

The majority opinion of Justice Douglas in the *Cleveland* case proceeds along the lines set by the prosecution in *Caminetti*. The problem was the application of "any other immoral purposes." The phrase was not limited to sexual relations for hire even though the Act was aimed primarily at the white-slave business. Prostitution suggested sexual relations for hire; not so debauchery. Therefore under the *ejusdem generis* rule, while the general words could not be used to enlarge the class, they could not be more narrowly confined than the class of which they are a part. Polygamous practices "have long been branded as immoral in the law. . . . They have been outlawed in our society." They had been called by the Court "contrary to the spirit of Christianity and of the civilization which Christianity has produced in the modern world." Religion would not protect the defendants; Congress had provided the standard of immorality. While the majority opinion does not explicitly say so, the test is the wide one of *Caminetti*. The Court said it would not "stop to reexamine the *Caminetti* case to determine whether the Act was proper-

[108] 329 U.S. 14 (1946).

ly applied to the facts there presented. But we adhere to its holding, which has been in force for almost thirty years, that the Act, while primarily aimed at the use of interstate commerce for the purpose of commercialized sex, is not restricted to that end." But the Court actually did more. It took *Caminetti* in its widest sweep.

The dissent of Justice Murphy was to be expected. The age of the *Caminetti* case did "not justify its continued existence. Stare decisis does not require a court to perpetuate a wrong for which it was responsible." Moreover, the *Caminetti* case could be factually distinguished. Polygamy was after all a form of marriage. The form of marriage before the Court was "basically a cultural institution rooted deeply in the religious beliefs and social mores of those societies in which it appears." It was certainly not in the same genus as " 'prostitution,' 'debauchery' and words of that ilk." Presumably Justices Black and Jackson saw a similar distinction, for they also dissented on the ground that "affirmance requires extension of the rule announced in the *Caminetti* case and that the correctness of that rule is so dubious that it should at least be restricted to its particular facts."

The problem of the legal process was explicitly discussed in a concurring opinion by Justice Rutledge. He did not think it would be possible "rationally to reverse the convictions, at the same time adhering to *Caminetti* and later decisions perpetuating its ruling." He thought the *Caminetti* case had been wrongly decided. At least it had "extended the Mann Act's coverage beyond the congressional intent and purpose, as the dissenting opinion of Mr. Justice McKenna convincingly demonstrated." But the *Caminetti* case "has not been overruled and has the force of law until a majority of this Court may concur in the view that this should be done and take action to that effect. This not having been done, I acquiesce in the Court's decision." He did not say why.

But Justice Rutledge did indicate that the Court was free to overrule *Caminetti*. This was not an instance where it was proper for the Court to "shift to Congress the responsibility for perpetuating the Court's error." Apparently this shift of responsibility would be equivalent to saying that the silence of Congress was consent to the erroneous interpretation. But the silence of Congress should not always be taken as approval. The failure of Congress to repudiate misconstruction might be due to the "sheer pressure of other and more important business. At times, political considerations may work to forbid taking corrective action. And in such cases, as well as others, there may be a strong and proper tendency to trust to the courts to correct their own errors." He doubted whether "majorities could have been mustered in approval of the *Caminetti* case at any time since it was rendered." It was true that two bills had been introduced to limit the effect of the *Caminetti* case and "neither was reported out of committee." But "in such circumstances the failure of Congress to amend the Act raises no presumption as to its intent."

The history of the Mann Act shows the ambiguity of legislative intent. The ambiguity is partially resolved by a decisive interpretation given to the Act in the *Caminetti* case. The words used by the Court in that case are not mere dictum. They gave direction to the Act. The direction has been followed. The restriction thus placed upon the freedom of the Court to realign cases sets legislative interpretation apart from the development of case law.

The dissenting judges have complained about the loss of freedom. Twice during his discussion of the silence of Congress, Justice Rutledge suggested that the reader should look at *Girouard v. United States.*[109] The reference was to another

---

[109] 328 U.S. 61 (1946); cf. Special Equipment Co. v. Coe, 324 U.S. 370 (1945). There are related problems. The theory of statutory interpretation advanced here would restrict the ability of the Court to develop the law outside of the statute through case law, if prior interpretations have set the

majority opinion written by Justice Douglas. The problem there was the application of the Naturalization Act to an alien who refused to bear arms. The Court had previously held, in opinions much criticized, that such persons were barred from citizenship. The Court disagreed with the interpretation set forth by the prior cases. It stated, "As an original proposition, we could not agree with that rule." It referred to a subsequent act for its bearing on the intent of Congress. The method was one which had previously been used by Justice Frankfurter in the *Hutcheson* case.[110] Both the *Girouard* and the *Hutcheson* cases may be thought to involve great principles. One deals with the right of labor to organize; *Girouard* deals with a question basic to civil liberties. And in both cases the Court reversed its prior interpretation of a statute. The temptation to do so was strong. As Justice Douglas stated, "The history of the 1940 Act is at most equivocal." But he had already indicated that it was a substantial re-enactment of the provisions involved of the prior act, which had been interpreted differently. The opinion continues: "The silence of Congress and its inaction are as consistent with a desire to leave the problem fluid as they are with an adoption by silence of the rule of those cases." As to this the Chief Justice in his dissent replied, "For us to make such an assumption is to discourage, if not to deny legislative responsibility."

The Chief Justice saw no constitutional question. "No question of the constitutional power of Congress to withhold

---

direction so that the statute covered the field. See President and Directors of Manhattan Co. v. Morgan, 242 N.Y. 38 (1926); cf. International News Service v. Associated Press, 248 U.S. 215 (1918). When a statute is interpreted to refer to whatever area of power is granted by the Constitution, the statute changes as the Constitution changes. See United States v. South-Eastern Underwriters Ass'n, 322 U.S. 533 (1944); cf. Helvering v. Griffiths, 318 U.S. 371 (1943), and Montana Horse Products Co. v. Great Northern Ry. Co., 91 Mont. 194 (1932); see Lyon, Old Statutes and New Constitution, 44 Col. L. Rev. 599 (1944).

110 United States v. Hutcheson, 312 U.S. 219 (1941).

citizenship on these grounds was involved. That power was not doubted." But perhaps the justification for the majority opinion is its oblique reference to the Constitution. "The struggle for religious liberty," wrote Justice Douglas, "has through the centuries been an effort to accommodate the demands of the State to the conscience of the individual. The victory for freedom of thought recorded in our Bill of Rights recognizes that in the domain of conscience there is a moral power higher than the State. Throughout the ages men have suffered death rather than subordinate their allegiance to God to the authority of the State. Freedom of religion guaranteed by the First Amendment is the product of that struggle." To be sure, the opinion does not rest on the Constitution. Rather its direction was, "We do not believe the Congress intended to reverse that policy when it came to draft the naturalization oath. Such an abrupt and radical departure from our traditions should not be implied."

But the appeal to the Constitution is important. Ordinarily a principle to be great enough to justify a reversal of legislative interpretation must be a matter for the Constitution. "Stare decisis is usually the wise policy," wrote Justice Brandeis, and "this is commonly true even when the error is a matter of serious concern, provided correction can be had by legislation."[111] Even when such correction could be had, the Constitution might justify a change in position by the Court. In *Erie v. Tompkins*,[112] Justice Brandeis held the Judi-

[111] Burnet v. Coronado Oil & Gas Co., 285 U.S. 393, 406 (1931); Helvering v. Hallock, 309 U.S. 106 (1940); Wright v. Union Central Ins. Co., 311 U.S. 273, 280 (1940); United States v. Line Material Corp., 68 S.Ct. 550 (1948); cf. U.S. v. South Buffalo Ry. Co., 333 U.S. 771 (1948); Commissioner of Internal Revenue v. Estate of Church, 335 U.S. 632 (1949); Douglas, Stare Decisis, 49 Col. L. Rev. 735 (1949).

[112] 304 U.S. 64 (1938); see Clark, State Law in the Federal Courts: The Brooding Omnipresence of Erie v. Tompkins, 55 Yale L. J. 267 (1946); cf. opinion of Chief Justice Stone in United States v. South-Eastern Underwriters Ass'n, 322 U.S. 533, 579 (1944).

ciary Act to have been incorrectly interpreted. The opinion rests in part on the research of a "competent scholar" as to the intent of Congress—an extraordinary step. But Justice Brandeis was careful to say that the erroneous doctrine would not be abandoned if it were only a matter of statutory interpretation. It was the "unconstitutionality of the course pursued" which "compels us to do so."

It is not that the silence of Congress implies anything. It is a problem of responsibility and effective action. To say that the matter must be one which involves the Constitution before the Court may reverse the interpretation of legislation places the responsibility where it belongs. But it still leaves open the path for judicial action if the matter is thought vital.

The doctrine of finality for prior decisions setting the course for the interpretation of a statute is not always followed. Moreover, the appeal to the Constitution which the doctrine compels may seem to be spurious, if it is viewed as a matter of constitutional construction, not because the construction of the Constitution is wrong, but because the appeal is made in such a manner as to avoid any construction. Nevertheless, the doctrine remains as more than descriptive. More than any other doctrine in the field of precedent, it has served to limit the freedom of the court. It marks an essential difference between statutory interpretation on the one hand and case law and constitutional interpretation on the other.

IV

The written Constitution in the United States has been much discussed for the power which the Court says it has been given to invalidate legislative acts. In words reminiscent of Chief Justice Marshall's language in *Marbury v. Madison*,[113] Justice Roberts explained the process as one in which the article of the Constitution is laid beside the statute which

[113] 1 Cr. (U.S.) 137 (1803).

is challenged. The court then decides whether the "latter squares with the former." "All the court does, or can do," said Justice Roberts, "is to announce its considered judgment upon the question. The only power it has, if such it may be called, is the power of judgment. The court neither approves nor condemns any legislative policy."[114] But as can be seen, while the court neither approves nor condemns, in its exercise of judgment it does have to determine whether there is any connection between what has been done and one of the great ideals embodied in the Constitution. The problem of seeing connection is not so dissimilar from passing upon the wisdom of legislation as some have thought. If the proposal is one much talked about in the early years of the life of a justice, it may be easy for him to see the connection even though the proposal appears unwise. It is much more difficult if the proposal appears both new and foolish.

In addition to the power to hold legislative acts invalid, a written constitution confers another and perhaps as great a power. It is the power to disregard prior cases. "The ultimate touchstone of constitutionality is the Constitution itself, and not what we have said about it," Justice Frankfurter has written.[115] The problem of *stare decisis* where a constitution is involved is therefore an entirely different matter from that in case law or legislation. This is often overlooked when the court is condemned for its change of mind. A change of mind from time to time is inevitable when there is a written constitution. There can be no authoritative interpretation of the Constitution. The Constitution in its general provisions embodies the conflicting ideals of the community. Who is to say what these ideals mean in any definite way? Certainly not the framers, for they did their work when the words were put down. The words are ambiguous. Nor can it be the Court,

---

[114] United States v. Butler, 297 U.S. 1, 62 (1936).

[115] Graves v. New York, 306 U.S. 466, 491 (1939).

for the Court cannot bind itself in this manner; an appeal can always be made back to the Constitution. Moreover, if it is said that the intent of the framers ought to control, there is no mechanism for any final determination of their intent. Added to the problem of ambiguity and the additional fact that the framers may have intended a growing instrument, there is the influence of constitution worship. This influence gives great freedom to a court. It can always abandon what has been said in order to go back to the written document itself. It is a freedom greater than it would have had if no such document existed. The difference in the British practice is revealing. But this may say no more than that a written constitution, which is frequently thought to give rigidity to a system, must provide flexibility if judicial supremacy is to be permitted.

It may be suggested that the doctrine should be otherwise; that as with legislation so with a constitution, the interpretation ought to remain fixed in order to permit the people through legislative machinery, such as the constitutional convention or the amending process, to make a change. But the answer lies not only in the difficulties of obtaining an amendment, nor the difficult position of a court which obdurately refuses to interpret common words in a way ordinary citizens believe to be proper. The more complete answer is that a written constitution must be enormously ambiguous in its general provisions. If there has been an incorrect interpretation of the words, an amendment would come close to repeating the same words. What is desired is a different emphasis, not different language. This is tantamount to saying that what is required is a different interpretation rather than an amendment.

Thus constitutional interpretation cannot be as consistent as case-law development or the application of statutes. The development proceeds in shifts; occasionally there are abrupt

changes in direction. Within a period and a subject matter
there will be some consistency. The training of judges is reasoning by example in any event, and within certain areas cases
will be compared and developed. Consistency cannot be overlooked entirely. The word of Justice Roberts is evidence of
that. His change in vote produced one of the most dramatic
shifts in recent Supreme Court history; yet he later was to
complain that too many reversals tend "to bring adjudications
of this tribunal into the same class as a restricted railroad
ticket, good for this day and train only."[116] There will be
some consistency, but it is not the consistency of case law or
statute.

Differences are immediately apparent. Each major concept
written into the document embodies a number of conflicting
ideals. The commerce clause, for example, at different times
represents the virtues of home rule and the glory of the
strength of a nation. The conflicting ideas are represented by
satellite categories which interpret the written word. No one
satellite concept can control. The major words written in the
document are too ambiguous; the ideals are too conflicting,
and no interpretation can be decisive. The satellite words are
handled with a recognition that they involve the perennial
problems of government: the relationship between problems
of the person, the state, and property rights. In our own system the fourth problem of the distribution of powers within a
federal system is added. Case-law concepts deal with some of
the same problems but less obviously. There is an affirmative
recognition in a constitutional case that the problem is the
connection between what is sought to be done and the ideals
of the community. Connection and consequence must be argued. The emphasis on consequence makes the hypothetical
example more important.

[116] Smith v. Allwright, 321 U.S. 649, 669 (1944); cf. London Street Tram-
ways Co. v. London County Council, [1895] A. C. 375, 380.

Perhaps it is easier for the court to see connection when the problem does not appear controversial. Courts which will rebel against taking a step during a controversy (which makes all kinds of hypothetical cases seem important) may slide into the same position when a more minor matter is involved. The position will be the same if reasoning by example later on can make it so. If the problem is to show the connection to the court, then the Brandeis brief, which attempts to do that, is less significant than the general prior talk and the social studies which have already had an effect upon the community. To put it another way, the Brandeis brief is important, but not so much for the case in which it is used as for some later case when its analysis has been accepted by the community. The examples used in the successful brief of the Government in the *Fair Labor Standards* case (the *Darby* case) were similar and sometimes identical to those used in the unsuccessful brief in the *Child Labor* case. It was the community, not the briefs, which had changed.

The consequence of this is that a constitution cannot prevent change; indeed by permitting an appeal to the constitution, the discretion of the court is increased and change made possible. The possible result of this in some fields may seem alarming. It is only a reminder, however, that "ultimate protection is to be found in the people themselves."[117]

[117] Frankfurter, The Task of Administrative Law, 75 U. of Pa. L. Rev. 614, 618 (1927). The use of a written constitution to justify a change in position is illustrated by the United States position before the United Nations Security Council with respect to the enforcement of the partition of Palestine. The New York Times for February 25, 1948, quotes the United States Delegate:

"The recommendation of the General Assembly makes three separate requests of the Security Council.

"The first—(A)—is that the Council 'take the necessary measures as provided for in the plan for its implementation. . . .'

"We come now to the two following requests of the General Assembly as set forth in the resolution of Nov. 29. These invoke the wide peace-keeping powers of the Security Council under the Charter. Request B in the resolu-

The development in the application of a constitutional provision may be shown in terms of the power of the federal government to prohibit commerce. This was the constitutional problem raised by the Mann Act. In handling this problem the satellite concept of illicit commodities developed. The concept itself is revealing, for as will be seen, an illicit commodity is only an instance of a case where the Court is able to see the connection between the regulation or prohibition and the ideals of the community. And because the Court has been able to see the connection for some items, reasoning by exam-

---

tion asks the Security Council to consider whether the situation in Palestine during the transitional period constitutes a threat to the peace.

"The third request of the General Assembly—(C)—asks that 'the Security Council determine as a threat to the peace, breach of the peace or act of aggression in accordance with Article 39 of the Charter, any attempt to alter by force the settlement envisaged by this resolution. . . .'

"Requests B and C of the Assembly's resolution, mentioned above, raised constitutional questions of the Security Council's powers under the Charter. What are the powers of the Security Council? . . .

"Although the Security Council is empowered to use, and would normally attempt to use, measures short of armed force to maintain the peace, it is authorized under the Charter to use armed force if it considers other measures inadequate. A finding by the Security Council that a danger to peace exists places all members of the United Nations, regardless of their views, under obligation to assist the Council in maintaining peace.

"If the Security Council should decide that it is necessary to use armed force to maintain international peace in connection with Palestine, the United States would be ready to consult under the Charter with a view to such action as may be necessary to maintain international peace. Such consultation would be required in view of the fact that agreement has not yet been reached making armed force available to the Security Council under the terms of Article 43 of the Charter.

"The Security Council is authorized to take forceful measures with respect to Palestine to remove a threat to international peace. The Charter of the United Nations does not empower the Security Council to enforce a political settlement, whether it is pursuant to a recommendation of the General Assembly or of the Council itself.

"What this means is this: The Council under the Charter can take action to prevent aggression against Palestine from outside. The Council by these same powers can take action to prevent a threat to international peace and security from inside Palestine. But this action must be directed solely to the maintenance of the international peace. The Council's action, in other words, is directed to keeping the peace and not to enforcing partition."

ple has then been able to extend the category. The analogy to diseased cattle and to lottery tickets in the debate on the Mann Act was not intended to be humorous. Present-day minimum wage and hour legislation owes its existence in some measure to diseased cattle, drunkards, defrauders, prostitutes, auto thieves, kidnapers, and convicts, and to those who sought to control them.

The Constitution does not say that Congress may "preserve the morals of the community by making it unlawful to transport women across a state line for immoral purposes."[118] The language is simple and ambiguous: "The Congress shall have the power to regulate commerce with foreign nations, and among the several States, and with the Indian tribes." In the absence of some mechanism for achieving an authoritative determination, neither the literal meaning nor the intention of the framers can be decisive. Even if the words were to be applied in accordance with the meaning they had when written, they could be given a broad or narrow application. In later years "among" in its context has carried the connotation of "between," but throughout the period it has also meant "intermingled with"[119]—a term which might preserve or obliterate the power of the states. Commerce might have been used to "refer to the entire moneyed economy—to the processes by which men obtain money, whether by the production or manufacture of goods for sale, or by the exchange of goods produced by others."[120] It may have been used to include "the

---

[118] Carter v. Carter Coal Co., 298 U.S. 238 (1936), Brief for Government Officers 127. See generally Stern, The Commerce Clause and the National Economy, 1933-1946; 59 Harv. L. Rev. 645, 883 (1946); Hamilton and Adair, The Power To Govern (1937); Sharp, Movement in Supreme Court Adjudication: A Study of Modified and Overruled Decisions, 46 Harv. L. Rev. 361, 593, 795 (1933).

[119] Stern, That Commerce Which Concerns More States Than One, 47 Harv. L. Rev. 1335, 1347 (1934).

[120] United States v. Darby, 312 U.S. 100 (1941), Brief for United States 51–52.

marketing of the products after the processing has been completed" and not "manufacturing, mining or agriculture as such."[121] Perhaps it was broad enough to include the movement of goods, as a part of traffic, even though the goods were not what would be termed commercial today.

To some extent the understanding of the framers of the Constitution must have been to have a national government able to operate in "all cases where the States are incompetent" or "in which the harmony of the United States may be interrupted by the exercise of individual legislation." This was the Sixth Virginia Resolution, and it was adopted by the Convention. But the delegation of power to the federal government in the commerce clause, except for the word "among," which may make all the difference, bears a close resemblance to the defeated New Jersey Plan which was said to give to the national government "additional powers in a few cases only."[122] Indeed it has been urged that the commerce clause was "a negative and preventive provision" intended to bring about "freedom of commercial intercourse" by removing barriers placed by the states but without any grant of power to Congress itself "to prohibit commerce in legitimate articles."[123] The separate provision prohibiting the states from levying "any imposts or duties on imports or exports" and the failure to deny to Congress the right to prohibit from commerce the products of slave labor have been urged, in the one case for and in the latter instance against, a broad interpretation of the commerce clause.[124] To the necessary ambiguity of word and

---

[121] Stern, op. cit. supra note 119, at 1346.

[122] Ibid., at 1338.

[123] Madison, letter to Cabell, Feb. 13, 1829, 3 Farrand 478, quoted in Brief for Government Officers in Carter Coal case 177 (1925).

[124] Cushman, The National Police Power under the Commerce Clause of the Constitution, 3 Minn. L. Rev. 452, 459 (1919); Stern, op. cit. supra note 119, at 1345.

intention must be added the knowledge that some of the framers at least were aware that "there ought to be a capacity to provide for future contingencies."[125] Perhaps they expected the words to change their meanings as exigencies arose. Perhaps they realized that ambiguity was best.[126]

A decisive interpretation was required to resolve the ambiguity. A broad and a compelling opinion was given by Chief Justice Marshall in *Gibbons v. Ogden*. The case concerned the right of New York to grant a monopoly of the right to use steam navigation within its territorial waters, and thus raised sharply the problem of whether commerce included navigation and, in the context of this case, conferred exclusive power on the federal government. In stating that it did, Marshall said: "The subject to be regulated is commerce. . . . The counsel for the appellee would limit it to traffic, to buying and selling, or the interchange of commodities, and do not admit that it comprehends navigation. This would restrict a general term, applicable to many objects, to one of its significations. Commerce undoubtedly is traffic, but it is something more: it is intercourse. It describes the commercial intercourse between nations, and parts of nations, in all of its branches, and is regulated by prescribing rules for carrying on that intercourse."[127]

With navigation included within the field of commercial

[125] The Federalist No. 34, at 217 (Tudor ed., 1937).

[126] "Neither the Philadelphia Convention nor the discussions preceding ratification of its labors generated currents of important thoughts concerning the process of adjusting Congressional and state authorities. The records disclose no constructive criticisms by the states of the commerce clause as proposed to them. . . . The influential early commentators on the Constitution—the Federalist and Tucker's Blackstone—shed most flickering and ambiguous light on the reach of the commerce clause. . . . And so, when first confronted with the commerce clause, the Supreme Court had to evolve doctrines without substantial guidance or restriction by previous discussion and analysis." Frankfurter, The Commerce Clause 12 (1937).

[127] 9 Wheat. (U.S.) 1, 188 (1824).

intercourse, the problem was what was reserved for the states. The dividing line was given in these terms: "The genius and character of the whole government seems to be, that its action is to be applied to all the external concerns of the nation, but not to those which are completely within a particular State, which do not affect other States, and with which it is not necessary to interfere, for the purpose of executing some of the general powers of the government. The completely internal commerce of a State, then, may be considered as reserved for the State itself." The states had the power to enact inspection and health laws, which came to be classified generally as police measures; the national government had the power to control that commercial intercourse which concerned more states than one.

But even the broad interpretation by Marshall left much ambiguity. Apparently it might be possible for a state to assert a police regulation over a matter which from a different point of view involved commerce among the states. And the Chief Justice did not feel compelled to answer what would be the result if New York, for example, were to have granted a monopoly within its territorial waters, in the absence of any federal regulation whatsoever over the subject. Yet the direction in favor of national power was clear. But a constitution cannot be so controlled, even though the rule stated and the example were persuasive. Already satellite concepts were at work. The federal government could regulate if the item were included within commercial intercourse, the exchange of commodities or navigation among the states. The individual state had power to regulate if the item could be classified as a matter for inspection or health or a police regulation. Reasoning by example would work within these categories and would create new ones.

These problems were important in the eighty-nine-year span between *Gibbons v. Ogden* and the consideration of the

Mann Act. They were (1) what items and articles were to be considered as a part of the traffic of commercial intercourse; (2) what activities were likely to fall within that area which concerns more states than one and, therefore, within the orbit of the federal government; and (3) to what extent the power to regulate includes the power to exclude or prohibit. The facts of *Gibbons v. Ogden* gave only partial answers. To be sure, navigation was included within commerce. Universal understanding in America put it there, Marshall said. But there was no answer from the facts as to whether or not the federal government might prohibit navigation. What of the items or articles which might be considered as a part of the traffic? Did they include persons? This would be important later on in connection with the Mann Act. It had been urged that one who carried passengers could not insist that the activity was within the commerce which Congress alone might regulate. But Marshall said "no clear distinction is perceived between the power to regulate vessels in transporting men for hire and property for hire." The facts of the case, however, dealt with the regulation of vessels carrying persons as items of the traffic; persons as traffic were involved only in a limited sense.

Thirteen years later, when the Court in *The Mayor v. Miln*[128] passed upon a regulation of New York requiring the masters of vessels arriving from foreign ports to give detailed reports on the passengers, a change in the meaning of the categories was already apparent. The act, the Court said, was not "a regulation of commerce but of police." Beyond that, while goods were the subject of commerce, the persons were not.[129] "They are not the subject of commerce, and not being imported goods, cannot fall within a train of reasoning founded upon the construction of a power given to Congress

[128] 11 Pet. (U.S.) 102 (1837).

[129] But the point was being made to distinguish Brown v. Maryland, 12 Wheat. (U.S.) 419 (1827).

to regulate commerce." Perhaps more important, Justice Barbour, who in this at least seemed to be speaking for a majority of the Court,[130] said, "We think it is as competent and as necessary for a state to provide precautionary measures against the moral pestilence of paupers, vagabonds, and possibly convicts, as it is to guard against the physical pestilence, which may arise from unsound and infectious articles imported from a ship, the crew of which may be laboring under an infectious disease." The category of moral pestilence is thus announced as a way of construing the Constitution along with commercial intercourse, navigation, and police regulations.

But when New York and Massachusetts attempted to go further and to collect fees rather than reports for incoming passengers, the Court showed the majority had not meant that persons might not be articles of commerce. The acts were unconstitutional;[131] the transportation of passengers was classified as a branch of commerce. The acts could not be justified solely as "internal police regulations." But note the language of Mr. Justice Wayne:

But I have said the States have the right to turn off paupers, vagabonds, and fugitives from justice, and the States where slaves are have a constitutional right to exclude all such as are, from a common ancestry and country, of the same class of men. And when Congress shall legislate, if it be disrespectful for one who is a member of the judiciary to suppose so absurd a thing of another department of the government,—to make paupers, vagabonds, suspected persons, and fugitives from justice subjects of admission into the United States, I do not doubt it will be found and declared, should it ever become a matter for judicial decision, that such persons are not within the regulating power which the United States have over commerce. Paupers, vagabonds, and fugitives never have been subject of rightful national intercourse, or of commercial regulation, except in the transportation of them to distant colonies to get rid of them, or for punishment as con-

---

[130] See the opinion of Justice Wayne in Passenger Cases, 7 How. (U.S.) 283, 430 (1849).

[131] Passenger Cases, 7 How. (U.S.) 283 (1849).

victs. They have no rights of national intercourse; no one has a right to transport them, without authority of law, from where they are to any other place, and their only rights where they may be are such as the law gives to all men who have not altogether forfeited its protection.[132]

Moral pestilence, in other words, was a most important category. It might be double-edged. It might permit the states to regulate or exclude items of traffic which otherwise could be controlled only by the federal government. Perhaps this was only an extension of the idea of a police regulation. It seemed so obvious to Justice Wayne that the safety of the local community meant paupers, vagabonds, and suspected persons could be kept out, that it was a matter of disrespect to the federal legislature to think it would ever try to let them in. But the other edge of the idea might be that the federal government, if indeed it could not let such supposed carriers of moral pestilence in, could also lend its aid in keeping them out. If the United States were to do this, who could complain? Surely not the persons regulated or the persons who sought to bring them in, for the persons so tainted "have no rights of national intercourse; no one has a right to transport them, without authority of law. . . ." Moral pestilence, then, might be a most important category indeed. It could operate to confer governmental authority both on the states and on the federal government. An item might appear to be excluded from the commerce power for one reason or another, and yet be restored to it if it were a matter of moral pestilence.

The idea of moral pestilence, which soon would go by other names as well, would become increasingly important if the items covered by the commerce clause were to be thought of normally as articles valuable for barter and sale. Commercial intercourse might well seem to carry that connotation. Something of this reasoning in fact was behind the recurring

[132] Ibid., at 425.

idea, which was soon to vanish, that persons were not the subject of commerce. In a sense persons were like insurance contracts, which the Court in 1868 proceeded to say "are not subjects of trade and barter offered in the market as something having an existence and value independent of the parties to them. They are not commodities to be shipped or forwarded from one state to another, and then put up for sale."[133] A court reluctant to confer federal power could narrow the category of articles of commerce. Trade marks might be the symbols by which men engage in trade and manufacture, but that did not mean they were clearly within the commerce power.

"Every species of property," the Court pointed out,[134] "which is the subject of commerce, or which is used or even essential in commerce is not brought by this clause within the control of Congress. The barrels and casks, the bottles and boxes in which alone certain articles of commerce are kept for safety and by which their contents are transferred from the seller to the buyer, do not thereby become the subjects of congressional legislation more than other property." The language reflected a shift away from the broad powers which might have been conferred by *Gibbons v. Ogden*. In the face of such a shift perhaps the category of moral pestilence might be used to restore the power to govern. Perhaps it could be joined with a concept carried by other cases, namely, that of "business affected with a public interest," and some larger category eventually formed as a vehicle for interpreting both commerce and due process. The category then could have in it not only paupers, vagabonds, and fugitives, but grain and other necessities.

The satellite concepts so far were principally commercial

---

[133] Paul v. Virginia, 8 Wall. (U.S.) 168, 183 (1868); see also Henderson v. Mayor of New York, 92 U.S. 259, 275 (1875).

[134] Trade Mark Cases, 100 U.S. 82, 95 (1879).

intercourse, the exchange of commodities and navigation or transportation on one side, and inspection, health, and police regulations on the other. The category of moral pestilence did not yet include many items. In a shift away from federal authority, greater emphasis had been placed on the necessity that the commodities regulated be themselves the articles of value which were bought and sold. The case of *Kidd v. Pearson*[135] added another popular category calculated to interpret the commerce clause in such a way as to cut down the power of the federal government. Iowa had proceeded to regulate the manufacture of intoxicating liquor, and it did so without regard to the intention of the manufacturer to export the liquor when made. The article regulated was one to which moral pestilence has sometimes been thought attached. The rule could have been put merely in terms of a police regulation. But the language of the case went beyond. Justice Lamar put it this way: "No distinction is more popular to the common mind, or more clearly expressed in economic and political literature than that between manufacture and commerce." Undoubtedly Justice Lamar had as much right to rely on a distinction popular to the common mind as Chief Justice Marshall had to rely on the universal understanding in America in *Gibbons v. Ogden.*

The language of *Kidd v. Pearson* was used to popularize a new dividing category. Manufacture, as with the regulation of grain, was a "thing of domestic concern." Commerce among the states was now to be referred to as "interstate," including as examples navigation or transporation. Soon it would be viewed conceptually as a "flow" across state lines. It had already come to include thousands of persons crossing on a bridge connecting two states.[136] The phrase "interstate com-

---

[135] 128 U.S. 1, 20 (1888).

[136] Covington and Cincinnati Bridge Co. v. Kentucky, 154 U.S. 204, 218 (1894).

merce" itself incorporated the distinction between manufacture and commerce.[137] Interstate commerce involved articles "bought, sold or exchanged for the purpose of . . . transit."[138] Interstate commerce did not include, for example, the activities of businessmen in controlling the refining of sugar in the United States because "commerce succeeds to manufacture and is not a part of it."[139] The interference with interstate commerce in such a case was at least not direct. Manufacture as against commerce could be in a way of talking about indirect as against direct. Thus two new classifying words were added.

When an attempt was made to apply the federal antitrust laws to the local Kansas City Live Stock Exchange, the Court responded: "But in all the cases which have come to this Court there is not one which has denied the distinction between a regulation which directly affects and embarrasses interstate trade or commerce, and one which is nothing more than a charge for a local facility provided for the transaction of such commerce."[140] Yet the rule of direct or indirect left room to argue that what might have been local and indirect was transferred by intention and design into a plan to affect directly "the subsequent contract to sell and deliver."[141] Intention and design which made for directness was the way the Court could explain that it saw the relationship. But the rule of indirect was strikingly different from that announced by Marshall, who had reserved for the states in *Gibbons v. Ogden* only "completely internal commerce" and those actions which "do not affect other states and with which it is not necessary to interfere. . . ."

[137] See Stern, op. cit. supra note 119, at 1348.
[138] United States v. Knight, 156 U.S. 1, 13 (1895).
[139] Ibid.
[140] Hopkins v. United States, 171 U.S. 578, 597 (1898).
[141] Addyston Pipe & Steel v. United States, 175 U.S. 211, 243 (1899).

The satellite concepts developed for the interpretation of the commerce clause were numerous. To some extent they duplicated each other, as for example the rule of manufacturing and the rule of indirect, which for a time seemed to mean the same thing. But all in all the categories were a way of comparing cases from different points of view. The problem of what federal regulation was to be permitted did involve the relationships in a nation between the person, the state, and property, and, in a paramount way for the commerce clause, the distribution of powers between the national and the local government. The categories reflected these concerns, but they did so by offering comparison of cases on the bases of what types of property were involved; where did the action take place; what was the act—for example, was it transportation?—and what was the motive or intention of the actor.

Among the array of concepts there was the category of moral pestilence. It might not always divide state from federal power. Perhaps it would confer power on both. Justice Harlan had faintly suggested the approach in his dissent in the *Knight* case.[142] He spoke the language of effect on the buying and selling of articles which go into interstate commerce as opposed to manufacture. But he did more. This was no attempt, he said, "to strike at the manufacture simply of articles that are legitimate or recognized subjects of commerce." The point was somewhat more explicit in *Reid v. Colorado*.[143] The defendant had shipped cattle into Colorado without having them first inspected as required by the law of that state. The defense was that the shipment was a matter of interstate commerce and under the Constitution not to be regulated by the state. The answer was given by Justice Harlan not solely on the basis that Congress had not "covered the whole subject of transportation of live stock." "The

[142] 156 U.S. 1, at 34 (1895).   [143] 187 U.S. 137 (1902).

defendant," Justice Harlan wrote, "is not given by that instrument the right to introduce into a State, against its will, live stock affected by a contagious, infectious or communicable disease [even though the particular livestock may not have been so affected], and whose presence in the State will or may be injurious to its domestic animals." The position was in the tradition of Justice Wayne's dictum dealing with paupers, vagabonds, and fugitives. But it was now to become the basis for federal action.

The Federal Lottery Act[144] attempted to prohibit the carrying of any lottery ticket from one state to another. Perhaps its constitutionality under the commerce clause could rest on the concept of transportation since the tickets were carried interstate. Nevertheless, the regulation was over commercial articles; and was not a lottery ticket like an insurance policy —contingent and not in itself an item of barter and sale? If a lottery ticket were not a commercial article, and the point was made by Chief Justice Fuller in his dissent,[145] how was it possible "to transform a non-commercial article into a commercial one simply because it is transported, as, for example, an invitation to dine or take a drive"? "The power to prohibit the transportation of diseased animals and infected goods over railroads" was different, "for they would be in themselves injurious to the transaction of interstate commerce, and, moreover, are essentially commercial in their nature," but "nobody," according to the Chief Justice, "would pretend that persons could be kept off trains because they were going from one State to another to engage in the lottery business." The commerce clause could not be enlarged to take care of lotteries. "In countries whose fundamental law is flexible, it may be that the homely maxim, 'to ease the shoe where it

144 28 Stat. 963 (1895).
145 Lottery Cases, 188 U.S. 321, 371 (1903).

pinches,' may be applied, but under the Constitution of the United States it cannot be availed of to justify action by Congress or by the courts."

The case was difficult; it had to be argued three times. Not only did the statute regulate traffic, in an article arguably noncommercial, but the regulation was to prohibit.[146] The majority opinion by Justice Harlan spoke of "the widespread pestilence of lotteries." Lotteries once favored had "grown into disrepute" and "become offensive to the entire people of the Nation." The tickets were subjects of traffic and therefore of commerce. And if there were doubts as to the power to prohibit, "what clause can be cited which in any degree, countenances the suggestion that one may, of right, carry or cause to be carried from one State to another that which will harm the public morals?" The act was constitutional even though some might argue this would mean "Congress may arbitrarily exclude from commerce among the states any article, commodity or thing, of whatever kind or nature, or however useful or valuable, which it may choose. . . ." There would be time enough "to consider the constitutionality of such legislation when we must do so. . . ." Lottery tickets could have been regarded as symbols of local activity similar to manufacturing and particularly suited for state regulation. But "we should hesitate long," wrote Justice Harlan, "before adjudging that an evil of such appalling character, carried on through interstate commerce cannot be met and crushed by the only power competent to that end." The rule of evil of appalling character as a basis for national action was not as broad as that suggested in *Gibbons v. Ogden;* even so it was suggested that the rule would have to be narrowly confined to the regulation of things "useless or inherently harmful."[147]

[146] See Corwin, Congress's Power To Prohibit Commerce—A Crucial Constitutional Issue, 18 Corn. L. Q. 477 (1933); Cushman, op. cit. supra note 124.

[147] Bruce, Interstate Commerce and Child-Labor, 3 Minn. L. Rev. 89 (1918).

These were the years immediately before the passage and constitutional test of the White Slave Traffic Act. No one concept could pre-empt the interpretation of the commerce clause. The language was that of direct or indirect; commerce was transportation and becoming a "current"; the nature of the article regulated was important. Any argument couched in one concept could be answered in another. Nor could one interpret the commerce clause by itself; the Fifth Amendment could be urged, and now the Tenth. How much persuasion the concepts exercised then is hard to tell. They were a result as well as a cause—indicating whether the Court saw or failed to see importance and relationship. But the concepts would have persuasive influence and the cases decided with them would be of great importance for reasoning by example. For this reason the *Lottery* cases were important. A pestilence seen there had suggested a rule concerning public morals.[148] Other things could be compared to lotteries.

Harlan himself was back on the rule of direct or indirect the following year in applying the Sherman Act to common-stock ownership through a holding company of two somewhat competitive railroads.[149] He was answered by White in a dissent raising the flag of the Tenth Amendment, although White the same year saw no such difficulty with the imposition of a federal tax which might "destroy the business of manufacturing oleomargarine." Perhaps the obvious difference was that oleomargarine tended to "deceive the public." The dissent was ambiguously concurred in by Holmes, who then on his own accord admitted that Congress might regulate an instrument of commerce whose effect was only indirect, but this was to be reserved for "heroic measures." Strangely

[148] "It must now also be regarded as firmly established that the power over commerce, while primarily intended to be exercised in behalf of economic interests, may be used for the protection of safety, order and morals." Freund, Police Power 64 (1904).

[149] Northern Securities v. United States, 193 U.S. 197 (1904).

enough for Holmes, the intent of Congress seemed to have a bearing on the interpretation of commerce, for if the intent was, through the anti-monopoly law, to "disintegrate society so far as it could into individual atoms," then "calling such a law a regulation of commerce was a mere pretense." It would be "an attempt to reconstruct society," and "Congress was not entrusted by the Constitution with the power to make it. . . ." Nevertheless, it was Holmes who weakened the rule of direct by adding words to it. He applied the Sherman Act to a combination of packers.[150] Commerce among the states was "not a technical legal conception but a practical one, drawn from the course of business." The movement of cattle affected was a "recurring course" or a "current" and therefore commerce. The effect on commerce was direct; it was not "secondary, remote or merely probable."

The Court looked at social reforms reluctantly. It took pains to state that the Tenth Amendment prevented the national government "under the pressure of a supposed general welfare" from attempting to exercise powers not granted.[151] It held unconstitutional the First Employers' Liability Act because it was applicable to shop employees. Even Holmes seemed to agree with this narrow interpretation of the commerce clause.[152] The Government, itself, in its amicus brief had argued, and thus on the constitutional point really conceded, that "the act would no more apply to a purely local line of the company than to any other business,—the mining of coal, for instance. . . ." Harlan, who had seen appalling evil in lotteries, and therefore the existence of national power, saw no such connection between "interstate commerce" and the right to "membership in a labor organization as to authorize Congress to make it a crime against the United States

150 Swift & Co. v. United States, 196 U.S. 375 (1905).
151 Kansas v. Colorado, 206 U.S. 46 (1907).
152 The Employers' Liability Cases, 207 U.S. 463 (1908).

for an agent of an interstate carrier to discharge an employee because of such membership."[153] The attempt of Congress to force the separation of coal mines from ownership by those railroads who transported the coal had to be cut down.[154] The railroad could comply by selling the coal they had mined; then ownership of the mine and later transportation would be permitted. Otherwise, serious constitutional objections would be present, among them the argument that the regulation prohibited. There was some acquiescence by the Court in federal regulations. Minimum-hour legislation for railroad employees "connected with the movement of trains in interstate transportation"[155] and safety regulations applicable to railroad cars which moved not only in inter- but intra-state commerce as well were upheld, but this was because safety and movement seemed apparent.[156]

It was so much easier when it came to something like the Pure Food and Drugs Act. The act was severe. It prohibited the introduction into any state or territory, from any other state or territory, of any article of food or drugs which is adulterated. It was applied to cans of eggs, adulterated because they contained a quantity of boric acid.[157] The Court took the act in its stride. "We are dealing," said Justice McKenna, "it must be remembered, with illicit articles—articles which the law seeks to keep out of commerce. . . . There is here no conflict of national and state jurisdictions over property legally articles of trade. The question here is whether articles which are outlaws of commerce may be seized wherever found, and it certainly will not be contended that they are

---

[153] Adair v. United States, 208 U.S. 161 (1908).

[154] United States v. Delaware & Hudson Co., 213 U.S. 366 (1909). But see United States v. Del., Lack., & Western R. Co., 238 U.S. 516, 529 (1915).

[155] Baltimore & Ohio R. Co. v. ICC, 221 U.S. 612 (1911).

[156] Southern Ry. Co. v. United States, 222 U.S. 21 (1911).

[157] Hipolite Egg Co. v. United States, 220 U.S. 45 (1911).

outside of the jurisdiction of the national government when they are within the borders of a State." The power to outlaw articles of commerce was a restatement of moral pestilence.[158]

It was against this background that the Court considered the constitutionality of the Mann Act in *Hoke and Econo-mides v. United States*.[159] The Act sought to prohibit the transportation of any woman or girl in interstate commerce for the purpose of prostitution or debauchery or for any other immoral purpose. The defendant argued that "the power to regulate commerce does not confer upon Congress the power to regulate the morality or any other immorality . . . of citizens individually." It was pointed out that immorality was a "phrase broad enough to reach drinking, gambling, exposure of person, fighting, lying, profanity—in fact any frailty which the flesh is heir to." And even though "prostitutes, both male and female" are "generally and justly deemed immoral," they "are citizens of their respective states, with all the privileges and immunities possessed by any other citizens and one of their privileges is to travel interstate, regardless of moral or immoral intent at the end of the trip." Moreover, persons were not the subject of commerce, and it was up to the states, in accordance with their reserved powers, to deal with such local matters as morals and prostitution.

No trace of difficulty is to be found in Justice McKenna. In the first place the language of the Constitution was clear. "Congress is given power 'to regulate commerce with foreign nations and among the several states.' The power is direct: there is no word of limitation in it, and its broad and universal scope has been so often declared as to make repetition unnecessary. And besides, it has had so much illustration by way of cases that it would seem as if there could be no instance of its exercise that does not find an admitted example in some

---

[158] See McCray v. United States, 195 U.S. 27 (1904).

[159] 227 U.S. 308 (1913).

one of them." Unfortunately, "experience, however, is the other way, and in almost every instance of the exercise of the power differences are asserted from previous exercises of it and made a ground of attack. The present case is an example."

The regulation was like that exercised in the *Lottery* cases, and over debased and adulterated articles. "Let an article be debased by adulteration, let it be misrepresented by false branding, and Congress may exercise its prohibitive power. It may be that Congress could not prohibit in all of its conditions its sale within a State. But Congress may prohibit its transportation between the States and by that means defeat the motive and evils of its manufacture." Congress had power to prohibit "outlaws of commerce." "But it is asserted that 'it is the right and privilege of a person to move between States' and that such being the right, another cannot be made guilty of the crime of inducing or assisting in the exercise of it and 'that the motive or intention of the passengers, either before beginning the journey, or during or after completing it, is not a matter of interstate commerce.' The contentions confound things important to be distinguished. It urges a right exercised in morality to sustain a right to be exercised in immorality. . . . It is misleading to say that men and women have rights. Their rights cannot fortify or sanction their wrongs; and if they employ interstate transportation as a facility of their wrongs, it may be forbidden to them." The analogy of these cases was not affected, it was said, because women are not articles of merchandise. "The substance of the congressional power is the same." It was too bad Chief Justice Fuller was not around to see that "persons could be kept off trains because they were going from one State to another to engage" in something at least like the lottery business.

It was one thing to justify an act which sought to prevent the use of women as unwilling articles of trade; it was perhaps quite different to justify under the commerce power a prohibition against interstate movement by seekers after illicit pleasure. It would be at least more outside a word intended to "refer to the entire moneyed economy." The argument advanced by the government in the *Hoke* case, to be sure, was broad enough to cover both, placed as it was on grounds of public morals as distinguished from the economic affairs of the people. The dissent by Justice Lamar in the *Holte* case,[160] where the woman was co-operative, takes a somewhat different turn, however. He suggested, and Justice Day concurred, that if she were "voluntarily traveling on her own account," she would then "cease to be an object of transportation." The argument was a throwback to the old view that persons were not the subject of traffic. One might recall the language of Justice Barbour and Justice Wayne and suggest that the more willing and the more immoral, the more subject to prohibition the traffic would be. At all events the arguments were again advanced in *Caminetti;*[161] the Court responded by stating that "the authority of Congress to keep the channels of interstate commerce free from immoral and injurious uses . . . is no longer open to question." At least where a moral pestilence was involved, commerce was not a matter solely of economics.

From the prohibition of white slavery, which, of course, did not mean white slavery, it was an easy step to the prohibition of foreign imports of prize-fight pictures.[162] It was a small step to the closing of interstate commerce to false and fraudulently branded articles.[163] Yet here the article might be harmless in itself. How could Congress close the channels of commerce to innocent merchandise? The argument had been advanced in the *Tobacco* case[164] without even winning a re-

---

160 236 U.S. 140, at 146 (1915).

161 242 U.S. 470 (1918).

162 Weber v. Freed, 239 U.S. 325 (1915).

163 Seven Cases v. United States, 239 U.S. 510 (1916).

164 United States v. American Tobacco Co., 221 U.S. 106 (1911).

tort from the Court. Possibly the answer there was along the lines suggested by Harlan in the *Knight* case. Even innocent articles might be considered infected with the odium of monopoly and restraint. And so here Justice Hughes now explained:

> Referring to the nature of the statements which are within the purview of the amendment [the misbranding clause of the Food and Drugs Act], it is said that a distinction should be taken between articles that are illicit, immoral or harmful and those which are legitimate. ...But the question remains as to what may be regarded as "illicit" and we find no ground for saying that Congress may not condemn the interstate transportation of swindling preparations, designed to cheat credulous sufferers and make such preparations, accompanied by false and fraudulent statements, illicit with respect to interstate commerce, as well as, for example, lottery tickets. ... The false and fraudulent statement, which the amendment describes, accompanies the article in the package and thus gives to the article its character in interstate commerce.[165]

Thus by the use of adjectives, subjects could be made bad. Was there no limit to the articles which could be thus condemned, and as to which, in fact, all other distinctions dropped away, as, for example, the distinction between manufacture and commerce? Hughes suggested an answer:

> Finally the statute is attacked upon the ground that it enters the domain of speculation. ... We think that this objection proceeds upon a misconstruction of the provision. Congress deliberately excluded the field where there are honest differences of opinion between schools and practitioners. ... It was, plainly, to leave no doubt upon this point that the words "false and fraudulent" were used. ... Congress recognized that there was a wide field in which assertions as to curative effect are in no sense honest expressions of opinion and constitute absolute falsehoods and in the nature of the case can be deemed to have been made only with fraudulent purpose.[166]

Perhaps this was the very center of the problem of interpretation. It questioned the role of the expert. It might deny

[165] 239 U.S. 510, 516 (1916).   [166] Ibid., at 517–18.

authority where there was an honest difference of opinion and wait for the time when there was that universal understanding, to which Marshall referred, or the assumed unanimous reaction which Harlan described when lotteries were condemned as "offensive to the entire nation."

In dealing with a case involving intoxicating liquor, White explicitly made the category of articles transported controlling. Since the act of Congress in this case was in aid of state regulation, the argument had been advanced that to permit "state prohibitions to attach to the movement of intoxicant lays the basis for subjecting interstate commerce in all articles to state control, and therefore destroys the Constitution." The want of force in the argument, White said, "becomes patent by considering the principle which, after all dominates and controls the question here presented; that is, the subject regulated and the extreme power to which that subject may be subjected. In other words the exceptional nature of the subject here regulated is the basis upon which the exceptional power exerted must rest. . . ."

In *Wilson v. New*,[167] where White permitted federal regulation of hours and wages of railroad employees engaged in interstate commerce against the background of a threatened strike which would have caused "the entire interruption" of that commerce, he gave some examples. He spoke of the difference in the power of regulation "which may be exerted as to liquor and that which may be exerted as to flour, dry-goods and other commodities." The difference was shown "by the settled doctrine sustaining the right by regulation absolutely to prohibit lottery tickets and by the obvious consideration that such rights to prohibit could not be applied to pig iron, steel rails, or most of the vast body of commodities." But perhaps the categories were not unchangeably fixed, for White

---

[167] 243 U.S. 332 (1917); see Powell, The Supreme Court and the Adamson Law, 65 U. of Pa. L. Rev. 607 (1917).

took account of the threatened strike, not as bearing on the type of regulation permitted but on the power itself. It was a view in some contrast to the dissenting opinion of Justice Pitney, who in words reminiscent of Chief Justice Fuller, explained, "The suggestion that it was passed to prevent a threatened strike, and in this sense to remove an obstruction from the path of commerce, while true in fact is immaterial in law."

The Child Labor Act in 1917 provided a severe test for the meaning of the category of illicit articles.[168] The act was to operate under the commerce clause, by keeping out of interstate commerce commodities made in establishments in which "children under the age of fourteen years have been employed or permitted to work, or children between the age of fourteen years and sixteen years have been employed or permitted to work more than eight hours in any day, or more than six days in any week. . . ." Certainly the interpretation of the commerce clause was not then pre-empted by a category of illicit commodities. The clause had been applied to regulate unfair competition or monopolies. It had come to be identified more and more with transportation and as such it permitted the federal power to regulate the use of safety devices and rates in intrastate commerce where the effect was interstate. Yet the most promising justification for the act was that child labor was child slavery and like white slavery, and that the products of child labor were like lottery tickets, intoxicating liquor, adulterated articles, and goods misrepresented.

The Government made the argument.[169] Child labor was "in and of itself immoral in character." Child labor was "child slavery."[170] Its effects were to be found in dwarfed bodies and minds.[171] Steam and electricity had made it so that a

---

[168] Hammer v. Dagenhart, 247 U.S. 251 (1918).

[169] Brief for the United States 10, 42.

[170] Ibid., at 14.   [171] *Ibid.*

cause operating in one state is felt in another.[172] It was unfair competition, and state legislation was impossible unless the states advanced together.[173] A change in public opinion regarding child labor had occurred "like that in relation to lottery tickets."[174] Whether the articles produced by child labor were good or bad would have to be judged by their effect.[175] Misbranded food might be wholesome. While the manufacture in which child labor was used might seem local, "nothing is more essentially a local matter than prostitution."[176] The regulation of Congress was to protect citizens in receiving states and to protect the health of persons in competing states.[177]

The complainant, who had filed a bill on behalf of himself and his two minor sons to enjoin the enforcement of the act, argued that it was sometimes good for a young man to work. For example, his failure to work might result in starvation for his mother and sisters.[178] The power of Congress to restrict or prohibit could only be used where there was a "real evil and injury involved in an attendant upon the commerce itself."[179] The lottery, pure food and drug, and white slave cases involved this utilization of commerce itself. But "the product of a factory is not unsanitary or adulterated or unwholesome because it has been touched during the process of manufacture, by a child's hand."[180] "It is not once suggested that the man who consumes the product of child labor is guilty of an immoral act, as, of course, he is not. Immorality

---

[172] Ibid., at 16, 19. A witness before the House Committee on Labor was quoted as follows: "Session after session at our legislature we have been met by the cry from the manufacturers, 'State legislation is unfair. You ask us to compete with States of different standards. This interstate competition will ruin our business. If we must advance, let us advance together.'"

[173] Ibid., at 19.

[174] Ibid., at 10.

[175] Ibid., at 41.

[176] Ibid., at 61.

[177] Ibid., at 38, 40.

[178] Complainant's Brief 11.

[179] Ibid., at 18.

[180] Ibid., at 21.

being thus eliminated, and unwholesomeness having already been eliminated, it occurs to us this statement of a national interest is fanciful and far fetched."[181] The argument stressed the consequence of permitting the regulation. "It is abhorrent to many people that manufacturing processes should be carried on by underpaid hands." If this type of regulation were permitted, then "Congress may prescribe a minimum wage scale and forbid the product of a factory in interstate commerce unless such minimum rates are paid."[182] Indeed, many persons objected to the non-hiring of Negroes. Was Congress then to be permitted to ban the products of factories which refused to hire Negroes?

In a five-to-four decision, the Court, speaking through Justice Day, held the act unconstitutional. The matter sought to be regulated, the production of articles, was a matter of local regulation, saved for the states by the Tenth Amendment. Commerce was intercourse and traffic. It included the transportation of persons and property, but it did not include such items as coal mining and manufacture. There was no authority to prohibit the movement of ordinary commodities. The lottery tickets, adulterated articles, and women to be used for immoral purposes were different. As to them "the authority to prohibit" was "but the exertion of the power to regulate." In each one of those cases "the use of interstate transportation was necessary for the accomplishment of harmful results. In other words, although the power over interstate transportation was to regulate, that could only be accomplished by prohibiting the use of the facilities of interstate commerce to affect the evil intended." Here there apparently was no such use of commerce. The goods "shipped are of themselves harmless."

Justice Holmes did not agree. The lottery case showed that

181 Ibid., at 39.   182 Ibid., at 40.

commerce might be prohibited. And this might be done even though the indirect effect was to regulate a local matter, as with the Mann Act, the Pure Food and Drug Act, and the tax on oleomargarine. "The notion that prohibition is any less prohibition when applied to things now thought evil I do not understand. But if there is any matter upon which civilized countries have agreed—far more unanimously than they have with regard to intoxicants and some other matters over which this country is now emotionally aroused—it is the evil of premature and excessive child labor."

The simple and ambiguous commerce clause was thus interpreted by made-up concepts of equal stature: direct as against indirect; transportation, a current, a flow as against local manufacture. North Dakota could not impose regulations on grain bought in the state but for shipment and sale in the Minneapolis market.[183] The "course of business . . . fixed and determined the interstate character of the transaction." The federal government could regulate the stockyards, despite the *Hopkins* case, because "the stockyards are but a throat through which the current flows, and the transactions which occur therein are only incident to this current from the West to the East and from one State to another."[184] A strike of coal miners would not be a matter of interstate commerce, but it could be made so if intention and plan made it have a "direct, material and substantial effect to restrain" that commerce.[185] There was, in addition, the category of illicit commodities, despite the setback of the *Child Labor* case. The category would apply when the Court was sufficiently impressed with some evil, occurring perhaps only after the transportation had ceased, to think of the evil in connection with

183 Lemke v. Farmer's Grain Co., 258 U.S. 50 (1922).

184 Stafford v. Wallace, 258 U.S. 495 (1922).

185 United Mine Workers v. Coronado, 259 U.S. 344 (1922).

the commodity. Within a year after the *Child Labor* case[186] Justice Day had no difficulty upholding a statute prohibiting the order, purchase, or transportation of intoxicating liquor into a state where the manufacture or sale of the liquor was against the law. The federal act went somewhat beyond the state prohibition in some cases, but this made no difference, for the "control of Congress over interstate commerce is not to be limited by state laws." Liquor for some time had enjoyed membership in the class of suspected commodities. Reasoning by example might extend the membership.

The National Motor Vehicle Theft Act gave the category new meaning.[187] It made it a criminal offense to transport in interstate commerce a motor vehicle known to have been stolen. Surely an automobile, even though stolen, is unobjectionable. The point was urged by counsel for the defendant and with it this statement: "We think that when this Court upheld the constitutionality of the White Slave Law . . . and likewise the Pure Food and Drug Act . . . also the Anti-Lottery Act . . . it went to the very extreme limit which we may ever expect it to go."[188] The brief made it clear that counsel thought the Court had already gone too far. But it was "altogether too late to argue," the Government rejoined, "that while Congress may forbid under penalty the transportation in interstate commerce of an unobjectionable woman merely because of immoral purpose of the man in effecting her transportation, Congress is powerless to close the channels of such commerce to the transportation of vehicles known to have been stolen."[189] The Court, through Chief Justice Taft, agreed with the government. The rule was stated broadly: "Congress can certainly regulate interstate commerce to the extent of

---

[186] United States v. Hill, 248 U.S. 420 (1919); see Hamilton v. Kentucky Distilleries Co., 251 U.S. 146 (1919).

[187] Brooks v. United States, 267 U.S. 432 (1925).

[188] Defendant's Brief 16.   [189] Brief for United States 2.

forbidding and punishing the use of such commerce as an agency to promote immorality, dishonesty or the spread of any evil or harm to the people of other states from the state of origin. In doing this, it is merely exercising the police power for the benefit of the public within the field of interstate commerce."

The Chief Justice showed that the *Child Labor* case was different. "Articles made by child labor and transported into other states were harmless, and could be properly transported, without injuring any person who either bought or used them." The illicit article cases, on the other hand, were cases where "the use of interstate commerce had contributed to the accomplishment of harmful results to people of other States, and . . . the congressional power over interstate transportation in such cases could only be effectively exercised by prohibiting it." In fact, it appeared that the invention of the automobile itself was to blame:

It is known of all men that the radical change in transportation of persons and goods effected by the introduction of the automobile, the speed with which it moves, and the ease with which evil minded persons can avoid capture, have greatly encouraged and increased crimes. One of the crimes which have been encouraged is the theft of the automobiles themselves and their immediate transportation to places remote from homes of the owner. Elaborately organized conspiracies for the theft of automobiles and the spiriting them away into some other state, and their sale or other disposition far away from the owner and his neighborhood have aroused Congress to devise some method for defeating the success of these widely spread schemes of larceny. The quick passage of the machines into another State helps to conceal the trail of the thieves, get the stolen property into another jurisdiction and facilitates the finding of a safer place to which to dispose of the booty at a good price. This is a gross misuse of interstate commerce.

The colorful language was used by a Court which was not liberal in economic matters. Two years before it had held

minimum-wage legislation for women to be contrary to the
due process clause.[190] Commenting on Justice Clarke's resigna-
tion in a letter to him, President Wilson had written, "I have
been counting on the influence of you and Justice Brandeis
to restrain the Court in some measure from the extreme reac-
tionary course which it seemed inclined to follow."[191] A depression was arriving. By 1933 "at least thirteen million persons were unemployed."[192] The Court permitted Minnesota
to grant a mortgage moratorium.[193] It permitted New York
to impose a minimum retail price for milk over the unappre-
ciated objection of Justice McReynolds that it was not indicated "how higher charges at stores to impoverished custo-
mers when the output is excessive and sale prices by producers
are unrestrained can possibly increase receipts at the farm."[194]
The two cases delighted the *New Republic*. It commented
that "one of the happier by-products of the depression is the
fresh air of realism beginning to blow through the chambers
of the United States Supreme Court."[195]

But in 1935 the Court proceeded to invalidate particular
federal control over oil production.[196] It permitted the federal
government to abrogate the gold clause in private contracts,
but not without the dissent from Justice McReynolds: "The
impending legal and moral chaos is appalling."[197] Then in May
the act "establishing a compulsory retirement and pension

[190] Adkins v. Children's Hospital, 261 U.S. 525 (1923).

[191] Baker, Woodrow Wilson 117 (1937), quoted in Frankfurter and Fisher,
Business of the Supreme Court at the October Term 1935–1936, 51 Harv. L.
Rev. 577 (1938).

[192] Stern, The Commerce Clause and the National Economy, 59 Harv. L.
Rev. 645, 653 (1946).

[193] Home Building and Loan Ass'n v. Blaisdell, 290 U.S. 398 (1934).

[194] Nebbia v. New York, 291 U.S. 502, 554 (1934).

[195] 79 New Republic 4 (May 16, 1934).

[196] Panama Refining Co. v. Ryan, 293 U.S. 388 (1935).

[197] Gold Clause Cases, 294 U.S. 240, 381 (1935).

system for all carriers subject to the Interstate Commerce Act" was held unconstitutional.[198] The Act went beyond the permissible regulation of commerce which would be, apparently, the promotion of efficiency or safety in the operation of railroads. Justice Roberts' opinion boldly discussed matters of policy and psychology, as, for example, what the reaction of employees would be and whether they would be grateful to the railroads. Chief Justice Hughes dissented: "The fundamental consideration which supports this type of legislation is that industry should take care of its human wastage. . . . The expression of that conviction in law is regulation. When expressed in the government of interstate commerce, with respect to their employees likewise engaged in interstate commerce, it is a regulation of that commerce." Then applying the test of direct or indirect, the Court held unconstitutional the attempt of the federal government through the NRA to regulate the New York poultry market.[199] To have permitted directness here would have encroached upon the states, or, as Justice Cardozo put it, "to find immediacy or directness here is to find it almost everywhere." President Roosevelt characterized the decisions as horse-and-buggy day interpretations of the Constitution.

In an atmosphere increasingly tense, Justice Roberts the next year put the Constitution beside the attempt of the federal government to reduce farm acreages by rental or benefit payments and found that the latter did not square with the former.[200] While deceptively under the tax power, the Act was one "regulating agricultural production," and it invaded the rights reserved to the states by the Tenth Amendment. The reasoning by hypothetical examples was peculiar. The Act was compared to "an appropriation to an educational in-

[198] Railroad Retirement Board v. Alton R. Co., 295 U.S. 330 (1935).

[199] Schechter Poultry Corp. v. United States, 295 U.S. 495 (1935).

[200] United States v. Butler, 297 U.S. 1 (1936).

stitution which by its terms is to become available only if the beneficiary enters into a contract to teach doctrines subversive of the Constitution."[201]

Meanwhile, Mr. Justice McReynolds permitted the federal government to make it a crime for a kidnaper to take his victim, in the particular case a policeman, into interstate commerce.[202]

Two cases presented a striking contrast in the interpretation of the commerce clause. The first was the *Carter Coal* case.[203] The federal government through the mechanism of a tax and credit system had sought "to fix the minimum price of coal at each and every coal mine in the United States." Employees were to be given the right to organize and to bargain collectively. The act set maximum hours of labor and minimum wages. It was held unconstitutional.

The government in its brief described the act as one intended "to remove burdens and obstructions from interstate commerce." The causal relationship between wages and hours in this industry and interstate commerce was direct. "In many fields, wages constitute over 60% of the total cost of production and the remaining costs consist of items which offer little leeway for reductions."[204] But in any event the federal government could set the terms under which commerce could be used; it could itself control and restrain commerce. The brief continued:

Much of the legislation sustained by this Court as an exercise of the commerce power has, so far from increasing the volume of commerce or providing for its safety, actually destroyed it by prohibition without in any way tending to increase the volume or promote the safety

201 Ibid., at 74.

202 Gooch v. United States, 297 U.S. 124 (1936); see Stern, op. cit. supra note 192, at 671.

203 Carter v. Carter Coal Co., 298 U.S. 238 (1936).

204 Brief for Government Officers 37.

of commerce in other articles. . . . It does not say that the power may used to insure the safety of individuals traveling in railroad trains, or to protect the interest of shippers in not having to pay excessive freight rates, or to preserve the morals of the community by making it unlawful to transport women across a state line for immoral purposes, or to safeguard the health of the community in penalizing the shipment in interstate commerce of the pure food or adulterated drugs.

It could have been urged against the Pure Food and Drug Act that its objective was to promote health and that the Constitution nowhere confers upon the federal government any power to promote health; it could have been urged against the Mann White Slave Act that its objective was to promote morality and that the Constitution nowhere confers upon the federal government the power to promote morality; it could have been urged against the Motor Theft Act that its objective was to prevent theft and that the Constitution nowhere confers upon the federal government the power to prevent breaches of state law. In all of these cases, however, the Acts were sustained because irrespective of their objective, they were obviously regulations of commerce; and the fact that their objective was, in one way or another, to promote the general welfare did not invalidate them as regulations of commerce, but served rather to explain and justify the regulation.[205]

The brief reminded the Court that "We must never forget that it is a constitution we are expounding." "The test laid down by Marshall is thus not a historical one at all, but rather one which calls for the construction of the Constitution in the light of current conditions. . . ."[206]

The Court said it agreed with the Government that "the validity of the exaction does not rest upon the taxing power but upon the power of Congress to regulate interstate commerce." It was "no longer open to question that the general

---

[205] Ibid., at 127 and 136. At 143, the brief states: "the government has not emphasized or insisted upon the authority of cases like the Lottery Cases, Hoke v. United States, and Brooks v. United States because they go beyond what in this case the government is required to sustain."

[206] Ibid., at 186.

government, unlike the states . . . possesses no inherent power in respect of the internal affairs of the states. . . . Every journey to a forbidden end begins with the first step." Plainly the incidents leading up to and culminating in the mining of coal do not constitute "intercourse for the purpose of trade." No distinction was more popular to the common mind, it said, quoting *Kidd v. Pearson,* "than that between manufacture and commerce." It quoted the *Knight* case: "Commerce succeeds to manufacture and is not a part of it." "Whether the effect of a given activity or condition is direct or indirect is not always easy to determine," but it was not a matter of degree. The relationship of employer and employee was a local one.

The second case was *Kentucky Whip & Collar.*[207] It involved the constitutionality of the Ashurst-Sumners Act, which made it unlawful "knowingly to transport in interstate or foreign commerce goods made by convict labor into any State where the goods are intended to be received . . . in violation of its laws." The Court held the Act to be constitutional. Its constitutionality was attacked on the ground that the regulation was a prohibition. "It is well settled . . . that no such power to regulate through prohibition can be exercised with reference to useful and harmless articles of commerce. . . . Congress has no power to look beyond the article itself. It can consider only the inherently evil or harmful qualities of the article itself, or the evil or harmful uses for which it is designed."[208] It was difficult to see any harm in the horse collars and harnesses which the petitioner manufactured.

But the Court in a unanimous decision responded by showing how Congress might connect the article with an anticipated evil. At a time when the Court was strained almost to the breaking point against New Deal legislation, and had re-

207 Kentucky Whip & Collar Co. v. I.C.R. Co., 299 U.S. 334 (1937).
208 Brief for Petitioner 18.

fused to see any likelihood of anticipated evil in coal mined outside of imposed regulations, Chief Justice Hughes was able to write an opinion about convict-made goods which almost pushed the *Child Labor* case out of the books.

"The anticipated evil," wrote the Chief Justice, "may proceed from something inherent in the subject of transportation as in the case of diseased or noxious articles which are unfit for commerce. . . . Or the evil may lie in the purpose of the transportation, as in the case of lottery tickets, or the transportation of women for immoral purposes. . . . The prohibition may be designed to give effect to the policies of the Congress in relation to the instrumentalities of interstate commerce, as in the case of commodities owned by interstate carriers. . . . And while the power to regulate interstate commerce resides in the Congress, which must determine its own policy, the Congress may shape that policy in the light of the fact that transportation in interstate commerce, if permitted would aid in the frustration of valid state laws. . . ." Motor vehicles were themselves useful and proper subjects of commerce, but their transportation by one who knows they have been stolen is "a gross misuse of interstate commerce." Even intoxicating liquors, for that matter, were otherwise legitimate articles of commerce. The *Child Labor* case was different, for the "Court concluded that the Act of Congress . . . had as its aim the placing of local production under federal control." The category of illicit articles, now converted to one of anticipated evil, continued to ride alongside the equal category of local production. The *Carter Coal* case was in one; the *Kentucky Whip* was in the other.

Kentucky Whip was decided on January 4, 1937. On February 5, President Roosevelt proposed his "reform of the judiciary." The bill would have added a new justice to the Supreme Court for each justice over seventy years of age. The majority of the Court was under great pressure. Looking back, it appears that controversial issues had made the majority less amenable to a philosophy of increased government responsibility. Where the controversy was least, as with stolen automobiles or the products of prison labor, increased powers had been granted, even though the absence of controversy did not mean that such measures had the approval of a whole people. These cases would have been persuasive without a dramatic shift in the Court's point of view. In the long run, it seems now that a shift was inevitable. A written constitution could justify delay; its ambiguous terms could hardly prevent change as people saw problems in a new light. Causal connections which justified the change might not actually exist. The economic theories expounded by the Government in the *Carter Coal* case might be low grade, but they were believed. Education or the lack of it would change the meaning of words. When the shift came, it would not even have to be justified by a realignment of cases; reference to a "rediscovered" Constitution would suffice. The Court-packing plan made the shift more dramatic, but surely no more decisive than it would have been. As Professor Beard wrote in July 1936, "It is inconceivable that in 1950 the President and the Senate will be able to obtain justices, even among casebook lawyers who will look at economy and the Constitution through the eyes of the middle class practitioners of about 1896."[209]

March 29, 1937 was the day of the shift. On that day the Court upheld the Washington Minimum Wage legislation;[210] it stated that it was "unnecessary to cite official statistics to establish what is common knowledge through the length and breadth of the land." It upheld the Railway Labor Act and did so in its application to repair-shop employees. The decision was unanimous. Referring to the pronouncement in the Em-

[209] 87 New Republic 317 (July 22, 1936).
[210] West Coast Hotel v. Parrish, 300 U.S. 379 (1937).

ployers' Liability Cases that back-shop employees were beyond the reach of the commerce power, Justice Stone wrote, "Whatever else may be said of that pronouncement, it is obvious that the commerce power is as much dependent upon the type of regulation as its subject matter. It is enough for present purposes that experience has shown that the failure to settle by peaceful means, the grievances of railroad employees with respect to rates of pay, rules, or working conditions, is far more likely to hinder interstate commerce than the failure to compensate workers who have suffered injury in the course of their employment."[211]

The National Lawyers Committee, "organized under the auspices of the Liberty League and composed of the 58 leading members of the American Bar, had issued a comprehensive report contending that the Wagner Act was unconstitutional and represented 'a complete departure from our constitutional and traditional theories of government.' "[212] On April 12 the Wagner Labor Relations Act was held constitutional.[213] The National Labor Relations Board had found the Jones and Laughlin Steel Corporation guilty of unfair labor practices by "discriminating against members of the union with regard to hire and tenure of employment," and by discharging employees in order to interfere with union organization. The Chief Justice set forth the argument of the company. "The industrial relations and activities in the manufacturing department of respondent's enterprise are not subject to federal regulation. The argument rests upon the proposition that manufacturing in itself is not commerce." The Government had responded by portraying a stream or flow of commerce through the manufacturing plant. But it was not necessary to decide the case by analogy to stream-of-commerce cases. In

[211] Virginia Ry. Co. v. System Fed. No. 40, 300 U.S. 515 (1937).

[212] Steel, October Term, 1936, 12 Conn. Bar J. 51 (1938).

[213] NLRB v. Jones and Laughlin Steel Corp., 301 U.S. 1 (1937).

contradiction to the language of the *Carter Coal* case, "the question is necessarily one of degree." It was decisive that "the stoppage of these operations by industrial strife would have a most serious effect upon interstate commerce . . . it is idle to say that the effect would be indirect or remote. It is obvious that it would be immediate and might be catastrophic."

In May the Alabama Compensation Act[214] and the Federal Social Security Act[215] were upheld. "It is too late today," wrote Justice Cardozo, for the argument to be heard with tolerance that in a crisis so extreme the use of moneys of the nation to relieve the unemployed and their dependents is a use for a purpose narrower than the promotion of the general welfare." Justice McReynolds in his dissent appeared to characterize the majority opinion as a "cloud of words" and an "ostentatious parade of irrelevant statistics." Then the term ended. The membership of the Court began to change. Five new justices were added within three years. The Court had been reconstructed. Justice Frankfurter later proclaimed the fact of "an important shift in constitutional doctrine . . . after a reconstruction in the membership of the Court." But he then said "such shifts of opinion should not derive from mere private judgment. They must be duly mindful of the necessary demands of continuity in civilized society. A reversal of a long current of decisions can be justified only if rooted in the Constitution itself as an historic document designed for a developing nation."[216] The old categories and the same judicial technique remained.

The registration provisions of the Holding Company Act[217] and the Filled Milk Act[218] were both upheld in 1938. Both of

---

[214] Carmichael v. Southern Coal Co., 301 U.S. 495 (1937).

[215] Steward Machine Co. v. Davis, 301 U.S. 548 (1937).

[216] Graves v. New York, 306 U.S. 466, 487 (1939).

[217] Electric Bond and Share Co. v. SEC, 303 U.S. 419 (1938).

[218] United States v. Caroline Products Co., 304 U.S. 144 (1938).

them were based on the power of the federal government to close the channels of interstate commerce. Companies which failed to register under the Holding Company Act were denied the use of the mails and the instrumentalities of interstate commerce. The protesting holding company operated through its system in thirty-two states. Its subsidiaries transmitted energy across state lines. The lottery, commodity clause, kidnaper, and convict-made goods cases showed that "When Congress lays down a valid rule to govern those engaged in interstate commerce, Congress may deny to those who violate the rule the right to engage in such transactions." The decision was to have been expected even before the shift.

The same thing could be said of the filled-milk case. The congressional act prohibited the shipment in interstate commerce of skimmed-milk compounds, with any fat or oil other than milk fat, so as to resemble milk or cream. It was clear now that Congress was "free to exclude from interstate commerce articles whose use in the states for which they are destined it may reasonably conceive to be injurious to the public health, morals or welfare . . . or which contravenes the policy of the state of their destination." Affirmative evidence showed "that the use of filled milk as a substitute for pure milk is generally injurious to health and facilitates fraud on the public." The inquiries of Justice McReynolds into the rational basis for New Deal legislation had not been popular. It was not clear that this was a matter for the Court to decide. Yet Justice Holmes had inquired into the rational basis for the Sherman Act; Justice Hughes had distinguished the false and fraudulent from the field of speculation. Justice Roberts had discussed the psychology of railroad employees. Now Justice Stone seemed to agree that such an expert inquiry was proper. "We may assume for present purposes that no pronouncement of a legislature can forestall attack upon the constitutionality of the prohibition which it enacts by applying

opprobrious epithets to the prohibited act." Apparently there
had to be a rational basis. It was a view from which only
Justice Black dissented.

Mulford v. Smith[219] showed the shift. As a result of the
Butler case, a new act had been passed which permitted the
Secretary of Agriculture to fix marketing quotas for cotton,
wheat, corn, tobacco, and rice. Justice Roberts found the act
to be constitutional and did so without any reference to his
opinion in the *Butler* case. The Pure Food and Drug Act,
the Mann Act, the stolen automobile and lottery cases permitted
him to say: "Any rule . . . to prevent the flow of commerce
from doing harm to the people of the nation, is within the
competence of Congress." Here also there was a "stream of
commerce" and a "throat where tobacco enters the stream of
commerce—the marketing warehouse." It did not purport to
control production. The words were the same, but the result
was different. Only the dissent of Justice Butler showed what
the relationship used to be. The *Butler* case had showed that
the Tenth Amendment did not permit Congress to control
farm production. Here "punishment for selling is the exact
equivalent of punishment for raising the tobacco." This was
an absolute prohibition of commerce, and the cases dealing
with illicit articles, adulteration, immoral purposes, stolen automobiles, and kidnaped persons gave "no support to the
view that Congress has power generally to prohibit or limit as
it may choose, transportation in interstate commerce of corn,
cotton, rice, tobacco or wheat." The dissent reads like the
argument for Carter in the *Carter Coal* case.

In *United States v. Darby*[220] the shift resulted in the disavowal of the *Child Labor* cases. The Fair Labor Standards
Act operated in part through the prohibition of shipments in
interstate commerce of articles manufactured by employees
whose wages were less than a minimum or weekly hours

[219] 307 U.S. 38 (1939).   [220] 312 U.S. 100 (1941).

greater than a maximum. The opinion by the Chief Justice made it clear that it was the *Child Labor* cases which were wrong, and which, not having been followed, could now be overruled. It was as though there had been no recent shift but a mistake in 1918. No doubt one could say that from the lottery cases to the control over the marketing of agricultural products, there had been a steadily increasing acceptance of government regulation by prohibition and in this line the *Child Labor* cases were an exception. But the Court had swung back and forth many times from the broad view of *Gibbons v. Ogden*. At a much earlier date Justice Story had written, "The doctrines and opinions of the 'Old Court' are daily losing ground. . . . The doctrines of the Constitution so vital to the country, which in former times received the support of the whole Court, no longer maintain their ascendancy."[221]

The reversal of *Hammer v. Dagenhart* was appropriately accomplished by reference to the Constitution as a growing instrument, if cases show the growth. To this extent counsel for both sides should have been pleased. The Government had made a full-dress attack on the meaning of the commerce clause, showing, as it had apparently not realized in prior briefs, that at the time of the Convention: "Lexicographers, economists and authors used the term 'commerce' to refer not only to the narrow concepts of sale or exchange, but to include the entire moneyed economy, embracing production and manufacture as well as exchange." But the Government was also careful to point out that "the men who met in Philadelphia did not create an instrument fitted to cope only with the exigencies of their time: they realized that the Constitution must apply in a 'remote futurity' bringing contingencies . . . illimitable in their nature. . . ."[222] Counsel for Darby stated

---

[221] 2 Warren, Supreme Court in U.S. History 139, 140 (1932), quoted in Moore and Adelson, The Supreme Court: 1938 Term, 26 Va. L. Rev. 1 (1939).

[222] United States v. Darby, Brief for United States 11.

somewhat frankly that "the Constitution defies logical analysis" and advocated the use of "judicial gloss."[223] Pre-eminent
in the judicial gloss seen by the Court were the cases of illicit
articles: intoxicating liquor, white slavery, lottery cases, adulterated articles, stolen articles, kidnaped persons, convict-
made goods, and filled milk. These cases had done their work;
perhaps they could now be forgotten, for, as the Chief Justice
said, they pointed to a distinction between things harmful in
themselves or having some deleterious property and other
commodities—a distinction "which was novel when made and
unsupported by any provision of the Constitution." Indeed it
was a distinction which had long been abandoned. Reasoning
by example had expanded the category to include ordinary
commodities.

V

The examples which have been used to illustrate the course
of legal reasoning in the fields of case-law, statutory, and constitutional interpretation are related. The category of things
dangerous in themselves from the field of case law and the
concept of commodities in themselves evil from the field of
constitutional law are in a way the same. White slavery can
be included within them. The history of the gradual growth
of the inherently dangerous or evil category is a history of expansion through reasoning by example until previously innocuous items are included. The growth is a reflection of a
period in which increasing governmental control and responsibility for the individual were thought to be proper. No one
economic or social theory was responsible, although as
changes came about in the manner of living, the social theory
moved ahead to explain and persuade. The social theory then
became useful in explaining connections. The point of view

[223] Brief for Appelle 11.

of the society changed.[224] It could not have been planned; it happened.

The legal theories were not an exact reflection of social theories. The liability of a seller of a previously innocuous article was not enlarged because some economic theory said this would be appropriate. Rather the growth of inventions made it hard to distinguish, when reasoning by example was used, between steam engines thought unusual and dangerous in an early day, and engines that moved and were now commonplace. A change in the method of selling and in social life made it hard to distinguish between what had once been the small known group around a seller and the vast outside world. Since the difference could no longer be felt, it fell away. And similarly in the development of a constitution, increased transactions and communication made activities previously remote and local now a matter of national concern. When a wage earner in New York thought his pay was dependent upon the standard of living in Georgia, whether it was or not, a fundamental change had taken place.[225] And with the increased con-

[224] Many were impressed with what they regarded as a new sense of responsibility; see, for example, Sidney Webb, Social Movements in Cambridge Modern History 765 (1910): "The Bolton Cotton spinner of 1842 had no need to keep his children in health, or his house healthy; his wife could with absolute impunity let the babies die, the whole household was free, in fact to live practically as it chose, even if it infected and demoralized the neighborhood."

[225] United States v. Darby, Brief for United States 58–59: "As the markets of the manufacturers expanded beyond state lines, the technical processes of production acquired a broader commercial significance. The apprentice to a New York cordwainer in 1800 would have only a disinterested curiosity in the wages paid the Baltimore apprentice. Today the worker in a Massachusetts shoe factory knows that his earnings reflect the wage scales in New York, Georgia, Maine and Missouri. If the result is that the field of congressional regulation under the commerce clause is enlarged, the cause is not a change in what the Constitution means, but a recognition of the vast expansion in the number and importance of those intrastate transactions which are now economically inseparable from interstate commerce—of the unification along national lines of our economic system."

cern for what had been remote and local matters, prior distinctions between neighbors within and without the state began to fall away.

The emphasis should be on the process. The contrast between logic and the actual legal method is a disservice to both. Legal reasoning has a logic of its own. Its structure fits it to give meaning to ambiguity and to test constantly whether the society has come to see new differences or similarities. Social theories and other changes in society will be relevant when the ambiguity has to be resolved for a particular case. Nor can it be said that the result of such a method is too uncertain to compel. The compulsion of the law is clear; the explanation is that the area of doubt is constantly set forth. The probable area of expansion or contraction is foreshadowed as the system works. This is the only kind of system which will work when people do not agree completely. The loyalty of the community is directed toward the institution in which it participates. The words change to receive the content which the community gives to them. The effort to find complete agreement before the institution goes to work is meaningless. It is to forget the very purpose for which the institution of legal reasoning has been fashioned. This should be remembered as a world community suffers in the absence of law.